Gaming Trade

PERSPECTIVES

Series editor: Diane Coyle

Gaming Trade

Win–Win Strategies for the Digital Era

Rebecca Harding
Jack Harding

LONDON PUBLISHING PARTNERSHIP

Published by London Publishing Partnership
www.londonpublishingpartnership.co.uk

Published in association with
Enlightenment Economics
www.enlightenmenteconomics.com

ISBN: 978-1-913019-00-6 (pbk)

A catalogue record for this book is
available from the British Library

This book has been composed in Candara

Copy-edited and typeset by
T&T Productions Ltd, London
www.tandtproductions.com

Cover photograph by Dara Dorsman
Dara Dorsman Photography Ltd
www.daradorsmanphotography.com
@daradorsmanphoto

Printed and bound in Great Britain by Page Bros

Contents

Preface

From *The Weaponization of Trade* to Mutually Assured Destruction

That trade has been weaponized has become mainstream thinking. It is acknowledged widely that the politics of trade are now overriding economic rationales. This argument may have seemed like crazy sensationalism two years ago when our book *The Weaponization of Trade: The Great Unbalancing of Politics and Economics*[1] was first published. However, when a front cover of *The Economist* bears the headline 'Weapons of Mass Disruption' and its accompanying image is of a bomb falling through the sky with 'Tariffs', 'Tech Blacklists', 'Financial Isolation' and 'Sanctions' written on its side, the idea that trade has become a weapon in states' arsenals for the maintenance of national security is no longer just hyperbole.[2]

Now the competitive landscape has changed. China has become more dominant in global trade finance as well as global trade. When European industrial policy starts referring to 'our competitors' in relation to China, and when Angela Merkel begins talking about a 'strategic competition', as she did at the Munich Security Conference in 2019, you know the world of cooperative, global capitalism is feeling threatened.

This book's core argument is that trade is being used as a proxy in the global struggle for power and hegemony: not just economically and militarily but also technologically as part of an 'all means' approach to foreign policy.

Increasingly, the focus of the major powers has been on controlling a new technological paradigm that, as yet, no one truly understands. Technological change, starting with the rise of information and communication technologies (ICT) in the 1990s, is now accelerating thanks to digitization, the Internet of Things and a web of complex interdependency. In the words of Schmidt and Cohen, the internet is 'among the few things humans have built that they don't truly understand: it is at once intangible and in a constant state of mutation, growing larger and more complex with every passing second'.[3] This has profound implications for trade. Trade is the weapon with which this battle is being fought because it is the delivery mechanism for so much of this technological change.

For example, who are we buying from when we order an Uber?

On the face of it, we pay a local driver who is self-employed on a zero-hours contract. However, we pay through a mobile app which uses technology that may be American or Chinese, via a device that could be American, South Korean or Chinese. The money goes to a company that is headquartered in the United States but part-owned by Softbank, a Japanese investment company that also owns shares in Alibaba, a Chinese search engine. This is the world of global supply chains. The thing is, nobody really knows how complex these interdependencies are, or how much trade goes on in the digital world.

The World Trade Organization (WTO) estimates that e-commerce like this accounted for around US$27.7 billion in 2016, the latest year for which data is available at time of writing.[4] However, e-commerce is not the entirety of digital trade. There is, in fact, no formal definition of digital trade, although the Organisation for Economic Co-operation and Development (OECD) has a working definition: 'digitally-enabled transactions of trade in goods and services that can either be digitally or physically delivered, and that involve consumers, firms, and governments. That is, while all forms of digital trade are enabled by digital technologies, not all digital trade is digitally delivered.'[5]

If we are unable to define something, then we cannot measure it. If we cannot measure it, then we do not know what it is. If we do not know what something is, then, as humans, we tend to be wary of it and – more importantly – want to control it. Is digital trade dangerous and a threat to national security? Or does it present global opportunities for 'network' solutions that create benefits for everyone?

The opportunities at present are, unfortunately, hard to see. China accused the United States of 'economic terrorism' and 'intimidation and coercion' at the end of May 2019. The United States, in turn, accused China of not playing by the rules. Early in 2018 the United States invoked Section 301 of the Trade Act of 1974, allowing it to circumvent the WTO and investigate on national security grounds the imposition by China of between US$50 billion and US$60 billion in tariffs on selected US imports. As a result, China's trade practices – and particularly their perceived threat to US intellectual property – were deemed 'unfair' by the United States.[6]

This represented a major shift in trade policy. By invoking this piece of legislation, the United States had effectively accused China of breaching its national security. Similar accusations against Japan, Europe (specifically Germany), South Korea and its North American Free Trade Agreement (NAFTA) partners, Canada and Mexico, were to follow. In other words, even allies were seen as potentially acting through the trade system against America's national interests.

This has created a febrile atmosphere for global trade. Our book will show that trade disputes around the world are only about trade at face value. Underlying them all is a struggle for global power, influence and hegemony of the digital flows – and, indeed, the paradigm – that underpins the direction in which our lives, and our trade, is being driven.

The focus is, as ever, on power. The concept of 'hard' power will be familiar to many: it is the power that is created through coercion and is often, though not exclusively, achieved through military means. 'Soft' power comes from creating influence through integrative means, and it principally comprises cultural, social and economic strength. A third theory of power has arisen in the literature in recent years: this is the concept of 'sharp' power, which is the use of subversive means to attempt to influence social or political norms and values through communications technologies.[7] However, we argue that we have moved beyond all of these and are transitioning to a new type of power. Rather than compartmentalizing it into distinct categories such as military, political, economic or financial, we explore the notion of power that exists at the intersection of all of these: paradigmatic power. This is the control that derives from the digital transformation we are currently witnessing. It concerns data as well as financial flows and control of the internet. In other words, it is about the way we trade as well as trade itself.

We can only find a positive way out of this struggle for influence if we understand the rules of the game and how it is being played. That is our starting point.

Trade in the post-Brexit, post-Trump years

The central theme in our last book (published in 2017) was that the language around trade had become belligerent. By evoking a spirit of war and conflict, it turned partners into enemies, becoming increasingly militaristic and economically nationalist. This rhetorical weaponization contrasted starkly with the language of trade used over the previous 30 years, which had been about opportunities, communication, partnership and growth.

In part, rhetorical weaponization came about as an appeal to a disaffected electorate: they had seen the gains globalization brought to the middle classes of China but had not reaped any of those benefits themselves. Trade was being used as a compelling narrative in populist politics, creating a unified sense of nationhood, with other countries being described at best as 'competitors' and at worst as 'enemies across the table'.[8]

The use of such rhetoric pointed to a seismic shift in the role trade was playing in national strategy. Rather than being an objective of economic strategy, as was previously the case, trade had instead become part of national security and, in certain cases, military strategy. It was being used as a tool to coerce, intimidate and influence in a way that we had not seen before. This was explicit not only in national strategy documents and the speeches and statements of influential policy makers, but also in the restructuring, and even fragmenting, of the framework of international and national trade governance.

In this book, trade itself is not the central issue. Trade is a proxy for a much bigger power struggle, not just between economic and political systems but also between different technological systems. This book is about the battle for control of the new paradigm.

In a multipolar world, centrifugal forces are pushing nations apart with the very tools that should be holding them together. The rise of ICT allowed people to communicate everywhere and be informed about everything; but it also gave everyone and anyone a voice and sharpened the public's sense of unfairness and disadvantage, unveiling the haves and the have-nots of globalization. Globally connected businesses and financial institutions continued to grow after the financial crisis, much as they had done before. Yet growing trade, conflated in the public mind with globalization, did not appear to be putting food into people's mouths or providing them with secure jobs.

Most significantly, globalization has shifted the locus of power to economics and trade. This in contrast to the predominantly military power of the Cold War era that arose as a function of the military industrial complexes of the two superpowers, the United States and the Soviet Union. The weapons needed in the fight to achieve influence in the digital era are economic ones. So, trade has become strategic. It is no longer just a mercantilist defence of industries from overseas competition but a defence of national security interests against other powers. Trade is now the frontline in the pursuit of global power and influence rather than conventional military action.

At present, the war of attrition between China and the United States is set to define geopolitics for the foreseeable future. However, there are not just two players in this game: we must also include Russia and Europe as the world shifts from a bipolar to a multipolar system of governance, driven by networked technologies that are redefining the nature of international relations and trade. This technological interdependence means that the players, who cannot be assumed to be rational, are all connected in a way they have never been before, through the very globalization and technological change that they are fighting to dominate. This makes a trade war the economic, and even the strategic, equivalent of pushing the nuclear button: it is Mutually Assured Destruction.

The term 'Mutual Assured Destruction' was coined by the nuclear strategist Donald Brennan in 1962 and first published in *The New York Times* in 1971.[9] The acronym for Brennan's concept (MAD) is no coincidence – it was intended to illustrate the absurdity of pursuing a strategy based on annihilation. MAD follows the principle of the Nash equilibrium, which holds that in a game between two or more non-cooperative players, where each side is aware of the strategy of their opponent, neither side will benefit from altering their current strategy. To put this in the context of the Cold War, there was no incentive for the United States or the Soviet Union either to launch a nuclear strike or to disarm themselves due to the potential repercussions. In trade terms, this would entail neither the United States nor China abandoning their current trade war; a full-scale escalation would be too damaging to their interests, while retreating would give all the power to their opponent.

This book is a contribution to the process of understanding the state strategy behind global trade in the context of the digital paradigm. We look at the use of trade not only as an economic tool but also as a weaponized alternative to conventional warfare in the interests of national security. Trade has always been part of grand strategy. As such, it has also always been gamed (i.e. manipulated to gain strategic advantage). Yet to imagine this is all that we argue is to miss our key point: trade is now an *explicit* alternative to direct military engagement. What may have been implicit in the past is now overt. As Larry Kudlow, Director of the US National Economic Council, said during a recent address to the Export–Import Bank of the United States: 'You are a financial tool and a national security weapon.'[10]

The brinkmanship over the last two years has had the goal of recalibrating the global trade equilibrium around a US rather than a multilateral global agenda. As a result, we are seeing a renegotiation of power relations as the world transitions to a new order, where digital technologies, the Internet of Things, digitization and interconnectedness are the reality of commercial and personal life. This presents a bigger set of challenges than globalization. It is a paradigm shift; a challenge to both the role of the nation state and civil society itself. The tensions we are currently witnessing are a wake-up call: multilateralism has benefits in this new order that bilateralism does not, and there are risks of miscalculation in gaming trade – not just economically but also, given the interconnected nature of trade and national security, militarily as well.

In writing *The Weaponization of Trade*, it became clear that if we, collectively, carried on along this path, the consequences would be serious. It was not inconceivable that a conventional war would be the result of mounting distrust between countries. We urged politicians to pull back, suggesting, naively, that they show some restraint before allowing the genie out of the bottle.

More than ever, it is our strongly held belief that we are the problem as well as the solution: we the 'chattering classes', the 'metropolitan elite', the 'citizens of nowhere', along with the banks, businesses, governments and thought leaders who failed to explain and distribute the benefits of globalization to their readers, their customers and clients, or their voters.

The word 'globalization' has become toxic. However, as we argue in this book, trade is not globalization. Since antiquity, free and fair trade has played a positive role worldwide in the form of cross-cultural understanding, export-led growth, economic development and access to technologies, health care, education and products and services. The economic and social development of humans has always relied on trade, and learning, between countries.

Now, trade has become conflated with globalization in a way that suggests it is damaging to national interests unless it is done on national terms. It is viewed as strategic, an integral part of foreign policy, and as a zero-sum game. The term 'zero sum' means that the gains for the victor of a game are offset by the losses of the opponent and thus the net score balances to zero. We need the businesses and banks who facilitate global trade to show policymakers that this is not the case: that, as a foreign policy weapon, trade is dangerous – not only because of the risks of miscalculation that might trigger military conflict but also because such conflict hurts the very people that trade could otherwise help.

People need solutions, and politics is not the answer at present. The world is slipping towards an economically nationalist version of extreme populism that has echoes of the 1930s. There are no winners in a trade war. By focusing on how to make trade better – by defining the rules, promoting environmental sustainability in supply chains, developing standards and protocols around data sharing and digital trade, and recognizing the difficulties that populism presents and addressing its root causes – we believe that it is possible to escape the downward spiral we are currently in.

Trade is part of the human condition; using it as a weapon is not. We need to show that trade – which is, by definition, multilateral – is in the interests of everyone.

Chapter 1

Choose your weapon

> Today an inability to combine principles with pragmatism and make a compromise when required seems to have driven our whole political discourse down the wrong path. It has led to what is in effect a form of 'absolutism' – one which believes that if you simply assert your view loud enough and long enough you will get your way in the end. Or that mobilising your own faction is more important than bringing others with you ...
>
> This absolutism is not confined to British politics. It festers in politics all across the world. We see it in the rise of political parties on the far left and far right in Europe and beyond. And we see it in the increasingly adversarial nature of international relations, which some view as a zero-sum game where one country can only gain if others lose. And where power, unconstrained by rules, is the only currency of value.
>
> — Theresa May, 17 July 2019[11]

Why the role of trade has changed

In the years since the financial crisis, the tectonic plates of trade have started to shift. Trade is no longer just the ships, planes and lorries that move the goods we buy around the world or the services we consume, either physically or digitally. While trade still plays a fundamental role in achieving economic targets and promoting growth, in the modern era it is also a weapon of state strategy in the contest for international influence and power.

Why has this transition in the character of trade occurred? The answer lies in the 'absolutism' that Theresa May identified in her final major speech as UK prime minister. Powerful states are increasingly reluctant to challenge one another through conventional military means. In June 2019, the Arms Control Association estimated that, between them, the United States, Russia and China possessed around 13,000 nuclear warheads.[12] As a result, the potential for MAD has limited the prospects for direct military confrontation between the great powers. In an era of somewhat tenuous nuclear peace, the challenge for states is how to protect national interests and build power.

This conundrum has led to states pursuing an 'all means' approach to power politics, characterized by a blending of conventional military force with other weapons, such as cyber- and information warfare, and through a blurring of the lines between economics, politics and trade. For example, the alleged involvement of foreign powers in election campaigns, including Brexit, and the information wars in Ukraine have given rise to the term 'hybrid' warfare, which we explore in some detail in chapter 6. In other words, the traditional compartmentalization of political and economic means has become less relevant as states attempt to mobilize all of the resources at their disposal in the pursuit of political ends.

So, in this context, trade becomes one of the most essential components of state strategy. We show in chapter 4 that, through economic coercion such as the imposition of tariffs, sanctions and embargoes, trade can be wielded as a tool of hard power to achieve strategic goals. In chapter 5, we look at trade as a tool of soft power through integration. An example of this is China's Belt and Road Initiative (BRI), which, at face value, develops cross-border infrastructure projects and boosts neighbouring countries' economic growth to prevent conflict, while also extending China's influence. In chapter 6, we find trade being applied by Russia in a more subversive manner through the supply of arms and ammunition to prop up regimes and insurgencies, facilitate the transition of the state's economy to a war footing, build strategic potential for the future through the stockpiling of goods and enhance a state's military capabilities in order to subvert a rival state's interests.

This book, then, is about control of a new paradigm, and within this context trade is being 'gamed' by states in order to achieve their objectives. But what do we mean by this? First, a game is fundamentally about competition between rivals. It is about implementing a strategy as you attempt to achieve victory and, depending on the game you are playing, it is about augmenting your status while limiting that of your rival. Indeed, much of the rhetoric being used implies that competition for supremacy is being treated like a game among the world's political elite. For example, between announcing his candidacy for the presidency on 16 June 2015 and the same date in 2019, Donald Trump used the word 'win' 336 times on his Twitter feed – that is, once every four days.[13] Meanwhile, former Secretary of Defence James Mattis warned that if North Korea used nuclear weapons, it would be 'game on'.

Second, 'gaming' something can be understood as exploiting it to your advantage. A typical dictionary definition of the verb is to 'manipulate (a situation), typically in a way that is unfair or unscrupulous'. Here, again, Trump's rhetoric implies that he considers the approaches of other states (most notably China) to be 'unfair'. Between 16 June 2015 and July 2019, he has used 'unfair' and 'fair' 81 and 86 times, respectively, on his Twitter feed.

It was his dissatisfaction with the perceived inequalities of the global economic system that inspired him to impose coercive tariffs; these were principally directed towards China but also affected historical Western allies in a so-called trade war. This zero-sum, utility maximizing 'I win–you lose' approach is classic game theory and constitutes the third way in which we see trade being gamed.

Such thinking is not limited to US strategy, however. There is strong evidence that Russia and China are adopting a similar approach to gaming trade. This is a crucial point, since we argue that the trade conflict we are seeing can be explained in terms of differing strategies (derived from distinct cultural interpretations of strategy) producing divergent behaviours in those games. At its heart, game theory is all about understanding the behaviours of other players. By looking at the behaviours of certain states in their approach to trade in the modern era, we can see strategy in action – and we can also start to compile our own.

Game theory and why it applies to trade strategy

Trade and game theory have been analysed together for many years, both by economists and by political scientists. For economists, trade games are largely about countries' potential to gain from protectionist policies. The outcome – that is, the welfare benefits – of the negotiating process will depend on the extent to which the other country retaliates.[14] Conversely, in international relations, game theory has principally referred to conflict that, according to certain theoretical approaches, can be seen as inevitable, given the different value systems between people or nations.[15] This, fundamentally, is the realist/neo-realist theory of power politics, where survival in a hostile environment through the acquisition of power provides the motivation for action. Power is usually seen as both the means and the end in this equation: as something to wield and something to acquire. Realists argue that conflict and competition are immutable concepts and, thus, planning for the worst-case scenario is necessary. This usually entails building up military capabilities and increasing strategic competition across multiple dimensions of power.

If conflict is treated like this, then it can take any form within the remit of a nation's grand strategy – that is, economic, military or cultural. Actors will approach the negotiating process with a view to winning and will want to understand the best way to win the game by watching the behaviours of the other actor(s). In other words, argues Schelling, strategy – whether to promote a value system through economic or military means – will be based on a value system that could, in itself, be nationally specific. What is interesting here is that the definition of victory is not necessarily couched in terms of absolute victory but in terms of gains against a value system.[16]

Why a trade game now?

This starts to become interesting when we look at the struggle between the United States and China. Trade wars are 'good and easy to win',[17] apparently, so why are we stuck in a conflict of attrition between these two nations where both sides appear unwilling to compromise?

Many pages of newsprint and analysis have been given to the US–China trade war, of course, and whole teams of economists in banks, corporates, governments and the International Monetary Fund (IMF) have weighed in on the consequences of an 'all-out trade war' for global growth.

Yet all the economic predictions combined cannot come up with a number which, in the grand scheme of things, would dent the global economy that much. Bloomberg economists anticipate that the impact of this war on global gross domestic product (GDP) growth will be around 0.5% by 2021, the year in which it will peak.[18] This is a net loss of US$600 billion in global output. The IMF anticipates a loss of 0.3% in the near term.[19] It seems like a large amount of money when presented like this, but it is a small proportion of global GDP, which was around US$85 trillion in 2018. According to Bloomberg economists, the United States will see its trade decline by around 0.5% if a 25% tariff is imposed on all trade with China, while Chinese GDP is expected to drop by around 0.8% by 2021. Again, these are relatively small proportions of GDP, which, in 2017, was US$19.4 trillion in the United States and US$12.2 trillion in China.

So, we have to look further than just the economic data into the reasons why China and the United States – and, indeed, the United States and its allies in Japan, South Korea, Europe and North America – have been threatened with tariffs and a trade war. The truth is, this conflict is not really about trade at all. Instead, it is about the existential challenge being posed to the hegemony of the United States and its allies by the rise of China.

During the early days of globalization, the rise of China did not matter. The size of its market, the growth of its middle classes and the opportunities it provided not only to sell but also – thanks to a highly educated and enthusiastic workforce – to efficiently produce financial services and technology justified the expansion into Asia after the financial crisis. The fact that China's financial sector was less affected by this crisis because it was not as integrated into the financial system at this point had major benefits: businesses could carry on trading and banks could build up a local presence in markets where trade and trade finance had the potential to grow exponentially. Economists spoke of the 'new Silk Road' as the challenge that 'South–South' trade would pose to the Northern hemisphere.

Now it looks like we are seeing the return of West–West trade and East–East trade. Middle Eastern trade with Russia and China has increased proportionately to its trade with Europe and the United States. Similarly, trade has declined between Africa and the United States and Europe but increased with Russia and China. Meanwhile, China–Russia trade is itself growing rapidly, not only in oil and gas but also in communications technologies as well as machinery and components, including computing.[20]

This is not just about the movement of goods, however; it is also about the movement of services and the movement of digital trade and financial transactions to parts of the world that have very different ways of running their economies and innovation systems.

Ultimately, the present trade conflict between the United States and China has been instigated by an existential threat to the former's 'status quo'. The negotiating position of the United States is clear regarding what it perceives to be the risks: increasingly, the concern is about national security encroachment through the sale of Chinese-made-and-owned technologies, the threat of intellectual property 'theft' and how the rules of trade are enforced. As such, it is a far more wide-ranging strategy than the espoused desire to use tariffs to make China play by the global trade rules or to reduce the US deficit.

It is really about digital

The world has been experiencing a paradigm shift since the financial crisis. The speed at which digital technology has become an everyday part of our lives, both in a business and in a personal setting, is phenomenal. We expect to be able to use smartphones rather than cash to pay for our coffee. The Internet of Things is a rapidly approaching reality. This all points to the fact that trade is no longer just about moving oil tankers around: it is becoming increasingly digital, and the payments systems driving this trade are not necessarily in banks.

In the digital space, China is powerful. Its technology has built a rival system to that of the United States which can help with accessing 5G networks, improve the functionality of our smartphones and allow us to set the kettle so that it boils just as we get home from work. Alipay rivals Apple Pay across Asia; Alibaba rivals Google.

Alongside this, the political leadership in the United States has changed, and with it the country's attitude towards globalization. The Trump administration, in the words of *Financial Times* journalist Gideon Rachman, 'believes that America's central role in the global economy gives the country a unique array of coercive tools that it is only beginning to exploit'.[21] This is a neo-realist approach to foreign relations: one where power and size matter. Its neo-liberal political counterpart regards absolute rather than relative gain as the only measure of success.

Let us take a look at this thinking a little more deeply. For years, the liberal elite that gave us *The World is Flat* and *The End of the Nation State* built its international relations theories on the basis that technology and globalization would be benign, and that the natural outcome of any game would be mutually beneficial because it was in everyone's interest to collaborate.

Collaborative, or converging, models of the world are in stark contrast to the neo-liberal interpretation of technological power. Neo-liberalism in this context is the use of the free market to develop and agglomerate technological power. Such an approach was developed by Farrell and Newman,[22] who argue that the idea that everyone is working collaboratively is palpable nonsense. Instead, they say, technology (and, by extension, the algorithms which drive learning within that technology) create mutually reinforcing power 'nodes'. These are heavily concentrated in the US-owned financial and internet 'interdependencies'. They can also be 'weaponized': the United States has the capacity to shut down access to complete messaging systems. These networks are becoming more concentrated, and, with them, so is US power. Military power is just a part of this, and trade or technological weapons can be used instead of such power in a conflict that no one sees. As China builds into this space, this is where the real battle will be.

That is why we are at a particularly dangerous juncture in the evolution of the world's economy and foreign relations. The conflict is not about trade, or even technology or military power. Instead, it is about controlling the new techno-economic paradigm that we have seen emerging since the financial crisis.

What does this mean? At its simplest, it is a view of how technology develops and evolves along a continuum. As humans become dissatisfied with what they have, they seek to invent new things. This is Schumpeter's 'creative destruction',[23] the mechanism by which, through entrepreneurship and innovation, capitalism reinvents itself. Bringing this to the world stage, as technology develops, argues Carlota Perez, it begins to filter through into society and the economy, and even into the regulatory structures of the state. It begins to alter the way we do things and, as it does, it becomes a new 'techno-economic paradigm'.[24]

Typically, such paradigms have arisen every 40 to 50 years throughout history, and a new paradigm starts as the last one is finishing. In terms of today, what this means is that digitization itself represents a new technological long wave: this technology is pervading every area of social, economic and political life. There are features that are common to every one of these long waves: large corporates will materialize that embody the technology itself, such as Facebook, Amazon, Google and Alibaba; new global regulatory structures will emerge, such as Basel III and Basel IV after the financial crisis; and social unrest and labour disputes will become increasingly frequent.

Let us dwell on this for a moment. Just because the process is evolutionary does not make it smooth. Digitization, although it began developing long before the financial crisis, has really accelerated since the financial crisis. Such rapid social and economic upheaval is bound to cause disruption, if not conflict.[25]

So, it is possible to see populism as a reaction to this technological change. In the virtual world of instant communication and purchasing power, the individual is sovereign and has as much power as any other. This generates a world of uncertainty – 'the largest experiment involving anarchy in history' – creating a system that is not 'truly bound by terrestrial laws' and constitutes 'the world's largest ungoverned space'.[26] In the real world, however, the individual sees job insecurity, flat real wage growth and higher levels of indebtedness. Given this disconnect between the two worlds, it is small wonder that at a domestic level mainstream politics across the globe is in crisis.

How the great game of trade encourages populism

This brings our discussion back to trade. In a world of constant change, there is a risk that social unrest will threaten politicians, whose job it is to create a stable employment base, to ensure the welfare of those who cannot actively participate in the labour market, to make certain that schools and hospitals are well resourced to produce a healthy and highly skilled labour force, and to guarantee the peace and prosperity of the nation. Yet, where voters are disconnected or disaffected, as they have been since the financial crisis, what simpler narrative is there to mitigate their unease than a zero-sum one? We will export more. They will export less. We will win. They will lose. All at once, foreign and domestic policies are secure around one agenda: creating jobs and security back home by controlling international trade.

The logical outcome of this is the economic nationalism that we have seen with Brexit in the United Kingdom and the Make America Great Again (MAGA) campaign in the United States. Trading partners and military allies alike have become 'enemies'. Politicians use the rhetoric of war to create a sense of national pride through trade; they toughen their stance towards their adversaries and promote the idea that greater power and influence through trade is both achievable and rational. This is the essence of the trade game.

There are many who would argue that neither the Brexit nor the MAGA mantra is rational and that game theory does not apply here because the politicians leading the charge do not have obvious strategies and are changing their views regularly and unpredictably. A foreign policy edict (or threat) tweeted at three o'clock in the morning does not suggest a careful strategic approach to a trade game that involves understanding the opposition and how they will react in order to arrive at the best possible solution for your country.

This would be naive. America's constitution ensures that it is run by the institutions of the state. While it may be true that the president is erratic at times, the administration, and particularly the trade negotiators under Robert Lighthizer, are not. The principle underpinning the latter's foreign policy is neo-realist, that is, power is everything and states will act according to their own interests. The political doctrine that this begets is neo-liberalism: win in the free market – at all costs.

Similarly, a poll of Tory party members in the United Kingdom in June 2019 revealed that, despite the constitutional crisis since the Brexit vote, and despite the deeper constitutional crisis that a break-up of the United Kingdom would cause, 63% want Brexit to happen even if it causes Scotland to leave the United Kingdom; this number falls to 59% if it means Northern Ireland will leave. In addition, 61% want Brexit even if it results in economic damage to the United Kingdom, and 54% want Brexit even if it destroys their own party.[27]

To the liberal elite on both sides of the Atlantic this seems irrational. But it is important to understand in this context what 'winning' means. As noted above, a game can be won if it is a gain against a core set of values.[28] Those values can be anything from a desire to collaborate and cooperate to, as we are seeing in the current situation, a desire for control and power.

To reiterate, this power is not really about trade. America's hegemony is being challenged by the rise of China in the same way that it was challenged by the rise of Russian military power after World War II. The desire for military hegemony is still there, of course, but in the same way that nuclear deterrence created a (tenuous) equilibrium in the interests of everyone, so, too, has the current threat of trade or financial conflict become a disincentive to precipitous action by either the United States or China.

This is happening because the economic and technological transition the world is going through has rendered China an equal threat to national security, because its power is increasingly, and similarly, networked through its social, financial and economic reach. This is termed 'sharp' power by the National Endowment for Democracy: it is essentially an interpretation of power that is neither soft (cultural) nor hard (military) which uses communications mechanisms to gain influence.[29] This is a direct threat to Western interests that is coming not just from China but also from Russia.

In this book, we take the concept of power beyond 'soft', 'hard' or 'sharp' to talk about paradigmatic power. This is about controlling not only the military, cultural or ideational spheres but also data and the digital world – controlling the new techno-economic paradigm itself.

This distinction is important, because it extends the combat zone from a physical space to a digital data space. To return to Farrell and Newman: 'Cross-national networks don't make the world flat, they result in a specific and tangible configuration of power asymmetries.'[30] That is, the flows which operate in a digital dimension can themselves be used to gain power. In contrast to the theorists who saw a world of cross-border collaboration and opportunity as the result of ICT, and the accompanying globalization,[31] technology as driven by artificial intelligence and digital strategy is predisposed to accelerate the process of gaining power.

Farrell and Newman use the hubs and spokes system of the financial messaging service SWIFT[32] and the internet to illustrate how such inequalities are likely to increase and how power is likely to become concentrated as the very algorithms that are meant to enable greater distribution actually coalesce around existing nodes. For example, SWIFT is currently the means by which information is securely transferred between banks within and across borders. Some of these messages, the authors argue, relate to Iranian-based banks, and because of this they are related to transactions that may contravene sanctions against, say, Iran. After some pressure from the US administration, SWIFT has shut down this messaging service in Iran to ensure that it can continue to trade with its larger client-base in the United States.

In other words, because there is such a heavy concentration of financial messages and internet data in the United States (and to a lesser extent the United Kingdom), organizations will adapt their strategies to ensure they can continue to do business. This is currently a key source of US paradigmatic power. Although China's reach into this space is not yet as extensive, the fact that Russia's central bank has recently joined China's Cross-Border Inter-Bank Payments System (CIPS) suggests that there is an increasingly viable alternative, and one that circumvents US-led sanctions against Iran.

The United States' main source of power, according to Farrell and Newman, is its control over these interdependencies and networks, effectively, the SWIFT messaging system and the internet. As we have seen in the case of Iranian sanctions, the United States asked SWIFT to make a hard choice: either keep the messaging systems open to Iran and run the risk of being sanctioned too or shut the messaging systems down and align with us. Similarly, in the case of the internet and security: either work with Huawei to develop your 5G network, or continue to work with the United States and, in the United Kingdom's case, within the Five Eyes security framework. Five Eyes is an intelligence-sharing alliance that rose to prominence during the Cold War. The alliance is between Australia, Canada, New Zealand, the United Kingdom and the United States; the US administration has made it clear that it will not work with Huawei technology, thereby linking physical security and intelligence sharing to trade and intellectual property. The neo-realism is obvious: paradigmatic power is everything.

This is not to say that China could not react. While the United States is taking this type of approach, China is promoting its BRI and building its own technological capabilities. China's separate, parallel and equally networked transactions and payments systems have an increased capacity to agglomerate power in exactly the same way as the United States. In financial terms, though, China's obvious 'nuclear' option is to sell the US$1 trillion in Treasury bonds it holds. Of course, this would mean that the entire global financial system would collapse; but if it meant that its technology could continue to grow, who is to say this would not be a weapon China might use?

Structure of the book

The role of trade in the world has changed. It is not just a means for enhancing the competitive, or indeed comparative, advantages of nations, or a means of creating economic wealth and opportunity. Trade itself has become a tool of the 'all means' approach to foreign policy in the current struggle for paradigmatic power. This power constitutes control over the new emerging techno-economic paradigm, termed 'Industrie 4.0' in Germany: the fourth industrial, or digital, age. In this paradigm, control over information and data is key, and 'hard', 'soft' and 'sharp' powers combine to allow countries to exert their influence and coerce in many ways. This power struggle is beyond geopolitical, because it is not just a fight for land and resources but also a battle for power over data and information. The weapons being used are dangerous because they affect the peace and stability, economic security and environmental sustainability of the world as well as the welfare of the people who are most at risk if the global economic system collapses.

Some readers will by this point have reached for the whisky and aspirin; but at this somewhat bleak juncture it is important to remember that this is a description only of the way in which trade is being gamed and why. It is not a strategic recommendation.

Our intention with this book is to give some hope to the people that this dangerous game is going to hurt most: those who work 14 hours a day just to make ends meet; those whose children go to school in shoes that do not fit or are falling apart; those who work in businesses across the world that are holding back at present because of widespread uncertainty; and those who help to finance those businesses. There is a way out of the absolutism to which Theresa May referred at the beginning of this chapter if the international community, including the European Union (EU) and the WTO, can show the leadership that is currently needed.

Because the word 'globalization' has become toxic, as mentioned, we will try not to overuse it. Instead, we want to champion the benefits of de-escalating current tensions and look at multilateralism as a strategy for mutual security and economic growth through trade. We see this as a way out of the vicious cycle in which we find ourselves: the slow growth that creates a popular sense of unfairness and dissatisfaction with politicians; which, in turn, makes political, economically nationalist and absolutist extremes attractive; which leads to protectionism and uncertainty; and which ultimately leads to even slower growth. We can only achieve freedom together, as this is a shared global problem.

Our goal by the end of this book is to have a multilateral strategy that addresses the issues which are normally dealt with at a national level, such as terrorism, cybersecurity, economic well-being, global standing, approaches to the environment and increased social inclusion. We believe these messages are essential to provide a counterbalance to the neo-liberalism that is dictating policy at present.

That said, our approach does not aim to criticize the individual nations or trading blocs we use as case studies in this book. We must acknowledge that there are grounds for all positions being taken. For example, in the words of one trade expert we spoke with: 'this [is] really hard to say, but Trump is right about China when it comes to trade. It's been getting away with it for years – hiding in plain sight. It took someone as abrasive as Trump to say it – that's all.' However, it is equally the case, in the words of another financial institution, that 'the Belt and Road Initiative is just business as usual for us. It's what global business has been doing for centuries.'

In chapter 2, we look at the state of world trade at present. In chapter 3, we develop the idea that trade is strategic and being gamed. We follow this through in subsequent chapters with a closer examination and interpretation of the trade games that are being played in the United States, China, Russia and the EU. Our central theme is that the United States has effectively turned trade into a weapon of military strategy but it is actually lagging behind China and Russia in terms of the depth of that strategy. These nations have come to realize that trade can be used in this way to build coercive power. Trade is being 'securitized' by the use of belligerent rhetoric to justify policy action: in other words, it is being turned into a weapon of national strategy.

The biggest risk now is the effect this is having on foreign and domestic policies in other countries. The United States has warned its allies against working with Huawei, and the collaborative/strategic relationship that China and Europe were embarking on in 2016 is now weakening. The United States' negotiating stance towards China, Japan, the EU and the United Kingdom remains the same: the focus is on trade deficit reduction, increasing exports of agriculture and manufacturing, and currency manipulation. In other words, if the United States sees evidence of central bank currency manipulation, it can launch a trade dispute without reference to the WTO.

The EU is stuck between three powers and has its own challenges. Its trade position is strong, as are its supply chains, fuelling intra- and extra-regional trade, with a heavy focus on strategic areas such as engineering, pharma, aerospace, automotives and electronics. However, the fragmented political coherence of this region and its power to prevent further trade or technological conflict is threatened by its own desire to compromise and collaborate. As a new administration takes the reins in Brussels under the leadership of Ursula von der Leyen, the EU needs to acknowledge that its response to the tensions between the United States, China and Russia will define its relevance in terms of foreign policy for many years to come.[33] Its commitment to core values and consensus politics are good things, and its strategy must be to build on these while recognizing that its 'unreliable ally' may well be playing a zero-sum game. The EU is a regulatory superpower: it should ensure this is a strength rather than a weakness.

We conclude our book with a suggestion for international strategy. We find it impossible to conceive of a world where we do not take the behaviours of others into account, or where 'winning at all costs' means the poor, excluded and disaffected lose. Our approach is unashamedly centre ground. We focus on the need for greater regulation of data and alternative currencies, we champion free trade and we urge that the focus on sustainable trade is sharpened. The WTO needs urgent reforming and business needs a greater say in how it could work. Most of all, we are convinced that the only way out of this crisis is to fight the causes of populism via sustainable investments, humility and a sense of shared responsibility from the world's leaders: in business and in politics. In order for multilateralism to win, or even to reach a stable equilibrium, it needs to play bilateralism at its own game.

Chapter 2

Power play

> Now, in the coming era, all of the great powers want to avoid a major war with each other. But they will compete fiercely to gain an upper hand in ways short of a major war. They will engage in coercive diplomacy and military build-ups. They may use force against smaller countries and engage in limited proxy wars with each other. They will exploit each other's vulnerabilities in an interdependent world – economically, technologically and politically.
>
> — *Thomas J. Wright, 2017*[34]

As we have shown, the major economic powers are engaged in a strategic competition to maintain and build their influence in a world that has become interdependent through the processes of globalization. But this is not a book about globalization. The distinction is important, because it explains why the world of trade should be concerned. Trade is the movement of goods and services within and across borders. It is what businesses do, and it is what banks finance and governments enable through the institutions of the state. Globalization, in its latest incarnation, is 'all about information (electrons and photons) – processing them and transmitting them'.[35] While this may be the context and reality of trade as it is evolving now, it is not trade itself.

In this world, power is everything. It is tempting to claim, as many do, that there is something 'new' going on, but in reality any change is endemic to the human condition and to evolution more broadly. As humans develop in relation to the world around them, they create new technologies, new forms of organization and new politics to enable them to gain control. This sort of change can be taken for granted. Often, what is more interesting than individual eras is how the world is moving between them.

Understanding that we are in a process of transition between paradigms is key to understanding why this is a quest for power, to win the strategic competition. As Wright says, 'history suggests that instability is at its greatest in the early phases of a new paradigm, especially one involving strategic competition'.[36] As we stand on the brink of a new techno-economic paradigm, at stake are economic systems and control of financial movements, data and military power. All of this is driven by the process of digitization and the movement of data as opposed to just people, money and ideas.

This is why we are seeing strategic games now. During the Cold War, the nation state and all that went with it – tensions between superpowers, the military–industrial complex and nuclear deterrence – were easy to articulate. The bipolar world order meant competition was binary and clear: the United States and Russia would not blink, but neither would they use their nuclear weapons – because that meant MAD. However, an equilibrium could be reached where neither side 'won' as such but a form of stability and certainty was possible.

Once the Soviet Union collapsed, strategic power relations changed. Accompanying the end of the Cold War was 'old' globalization,[37] where information, people, ideas and finance flowed freely across borders. On the face of it, this shift – enabled largely by the internet and improvements in ICT – made borders between countries unnecessary and potentially irrelevant.[38]

However, as Stiglitz wrote in 2003, globalization put 'new demands on nation states at the very same time that, in many ways, it has reduced their capacity to deal with those demands'.[39] The ever-closer integration of economies around the world put power into the hands of businesses to optimize capital and labour flows across borders. This challenged nation states to become multilateral in guaranteeing their economic security simply to support their businesses, which meant that inequalities increased domestically while new entrants to the world trading system, such as China and South Korea, gained economic power.[40]

In reality, what happened during the period of 'old' globalization was simply that the United States became the hegemon. Trade was largely conducted in US dollars. Power shifted from the nation state and the military–industrial complex to civilian powers: effectively, large, global corporations. In fact, what was unique about this phase was that it was dominated by civilian technologies and civilian markets, not military ones.[41] Ideas and intellectual property flowed freely across borders as businesses took up the competitive reins, leaving nation states playing collaborative games to achieve the best possible rather than the optimum outcomes. Of course, many of these businesses were US companies, so the power of the nation state became embedded in its national technological champions, with the United States the clear winner economically and, arguably, strategically as well.

This focus on civilian rather than military power and the challenge it poses to the nation state goes to the heart of the transition and strategic conflict we are seeing now. Over the past 30 years, Russia and China could work with the 'liberal democratic model' because it was in their best interests to do so. The game was simple: embrace liberalism, and welcome business and interdependency, because you will learn the rules. Even if these nations could not win at the outset, they could learn how to win eventually.

The techno-economic paradigm approach helps us to understand the nature of the transition now, how it affects power and, therefore, how it impacts trade. We are moving into a world where information, and control of that information, will define who wins the strategic competition between nations. It is the technology behind economic flows, including trade, that is making this a strategic competition. Technology is pervading every area of our lives: how many times have you bumped into a fellow pedestrian who, like yourself, is reading a WhatsApp or a WeChat message as they walk along the footpath? How reliant are you on your smartphone's WiFi signal, even when you are on holiday? How much cash do you keep in your pockets today compared with even five years ago? This dependency has evolved; it has not been a sudden, seismic shift. We have gone from making a cup of coffee while we wait for the internet to load on our home computers to using our phones to switch on the kettle to make that coffee. This transition has been seamless: we have barely noticed it happening.

But such a transition is not without conflict, and that is what we are seeing now. Who owns and – more importantly – controls the data you generate every time you touch a keyboard or swipe a screen? Do we trade more information than we do goods and services? How is this priced, and how is payment made? Who owns the cloud that enables all of this?

What is happening now is a real shift in the nature of power. As recently as 2015, Tim Marshall's important book *Prisoners of Geography* pointed out that geopolitics is, by definition, the mechanism by which international affairs are decided. Geography matters, states Marshall: 'landscape imprisons leaders, giving them fewer choices and less room to manoeuvre than you might think'.[42] So, what if leaders are no longer competing for land and resources but rather for cyberspace and the electronic trade routes and flows within it?

The answer, of course, is that there is conflict. We are already seeing this as our institutions, social and economic interactions, privacy and laws all become opaque. In previous paradigms, we have seen industrial unrest; now, we see populism. We have witnessed regulations tighten on banks; now, we note their absence as non-bank companies enable digital payments. We used to worry about identity cards; now, we worry about identity theft. We used to think Russia and the United States would engage in a nuclear conflict; now, China and the United States are engaged in a trade war.

This conflict is all about power, which has, like the role of the nation state, become equally confused since the collapse of the Soviet Union. After World War II, the popularity of realist thinking meant power was simply understood in hard, military terms, with the United States and the USSR as the central power players. Despite its significant oil wealth, post-1990 Russia ceased to have either the hard or the soft cultural and economic power to compete in the same league as the United States in corporate or financial services terms. China's entry into the international markets was not really evident until after 2001, when it joined the WTO. Both Russia and China, as has already been pointed out, were happy to learn from the US-centric economic liberalism that dominated the world order; but, particularly in the case of China, the consequences of this may have been underestimated by the West.[43]

Since the global financial crisis, these power relations have changed. China is now more powerful than the United

States in trade terms, while Germany has slipped to become the third-largest trading nation. China also has an integrative strategy, pulling its connections and networks together using its large businesses, its geographical and economic connections through the BRI and its technological reach, alongside a small, but still significant, military. Russia's military power has strengthened and is supported by a hybrid strategy that combines cyberthreats, propaganda and digital media infiltration with conventional power. The United States maintains its coercive approach to power through military means and, increasingly, trade. These diverse strategies reflect the divergent perceptions of power at work and the different timescales over which the power game has been played.

Power in an era of interdependence is therefore not as straightforward as it used to be, and this is reflected in the strategies that we are seeing. The tools used to coerce adversaries are not the same, either: China and Russia are equally as driven by their desire to gain power as the United States, but they have chosen alternative routes and are using different means, sometimes separately and sometimes in combination, for getting there.

The lines between hard and soft power are starting to blur: one country's semiconductor export is another country's cybersecurity import. For example, when North Korea's imports of duals-use goods related to nuclear goods trebled between 2007 and 2008, it is perfectly possible that these were associated with improvements in X-ray technology for public purposes. The fact that North Korea announced the revival of its nuclear programme and conducted a powerful underground nuclear test a year later may just be a coincidence. In this fuzzy framework, dual-use goods – or rather, goods that are used for military or civilian purposes – are treated with suspicion, since their end use could be benign but equally could be malignant. The issue is how they are used, not what they are.

This is creating a new paradigm that is part new digital technologies and part the intersection between different types of power: hard, soft and sharp. The United States, for example, has the most hard power in the world, and soft (or economic and cultural) power to match. China aspires to have the most soft power and is building up its hard power. Russia's soft power is no match for that of either the United States or China, but its military capabilities are formidable. Crucially, all are competing for sharp power, which is the control of information, data flows and financial flows as well as their use. Effectively, these three countries are operating in the same intersection of hard and soft power but are competing for dominance in all three. We call this paradigmatic power, as illustrated in figure 1.

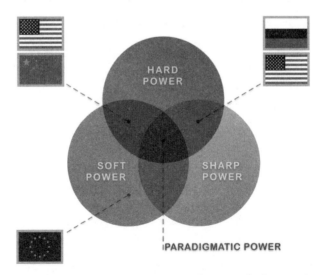

Figure 1. Blurred power distinctions and the struggle for paradigmatic power.

Russia has hard power as a legacy of its superpower status during the Cold War. It also has sharp power, as we have seen through its alleged involvement in the US election campaign[44] and in campaigns to influence the outcome of the United Kingdom's EU referendum.[45] While this is denied by Russian authorities, the fact that there is a suggested link itself speaks to the accumulated sharp power that Russia has. It does not have soft power, however, but it is building its economic and political links with China as a 'marriage of convenience' so that it too can play for control of the new paradigm.

Meanwhile, trade is being used strategically by countries to build their power bases. This is happening through trade weaponization in two ways: rhetorically and literally. The literal use of strategic trade is made explicit by the increase in arms and dual-use goods trading. Figure 2 shows just how important growth in arms trade has become since the United States shifted its foreign policy stance.

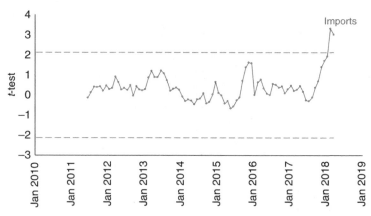

Figure 2. Arms trade growth measured in terms of *t*-test significance (above two standard deviations): June 2011–February 2018. *Source:* Coriolis Technologies, 2019.

This chart shows an annual moving average of trade growth in arms that is more than two standard deviations above the historical mean between June 2011 and February 2018. The sharp escalation in arms trading from mid-2017 to February 2018 is a function of not only hardening US rhetoric but also growing arms trading in other parts of the world, including the European states bordering Russia and the Baltic states. For example, there were significant increases in arms imports over the same time period in Finland, Norway, Sweden, Turkey and Australia as well as the United States. Meanwhile, China, the United States and, interestingly, Canada significantly increased their arms exports. This shows a marked tightening of strategy over the period studied that can be seen as a direct response to two things:

- The build-up of Russian military forces along its border with the Baltic states. Norway, Finland and Sweden all had explicit policies during that period to increase their border security. Canada, under the auspices of the North Atlantic Treaty Organization (NATO), increased its arms exports to Ukraine.
- The build-up of a Chinese military presence in the South China Sea. Australia's national strategy, published in 2018,[46] highlighted the importance of defence against the rising threat of China in the region. There was also significant growth in surveillance and security-related ICT.

The rhetorical weaponization of trade is present for all to see in the daily news. However, figure 3 shows the way in which 'trade', associated with military language in the news and on social media, changed immediately following the global shift in foreign policy stance. During 2017, the language associated with tariffs was mild, presenting the

United States in particular as a 'victim' through words like 'protect', 'hurt', 'terror', 'illegal' and 'massive'. By the middle of 2018, we can see that more such language was being used in connection with trade, but the focus had become harder, with words like 'tariffs', 'hurt', 'protect', 'unfair' and 'massive' becoming more dominant. The most dominant word of all, however, is 'war'.

Figure 3. The use of weaponized language associated with trade in social media and newsfeeds, January 2017–June 2018. *Source:* Coriolis Technologies, 2019. *Methodology:* The method employed here was to look at social media and newsfeeds using web-scraping and contextuality analytics between January 2017 and June 2018. The differential size of the boxes reflects the amount of contextual language used in each time period. Note that 2017 represents a full year of data whereas 2018 does not.

Apart from the fact that the world has become a more nervous place over the past two years, this analysis tells us two things. First, there was an escalation in arms trading over the period studied. This was directly connected to the tensions in 2017 and 2018 between Russia and its Baltic neighbours. However, Australia's trade in arms and dual-use goods increased significantly too. China used more belligerent military language and tactics in the Asia-Pacific region during the early stages of the Trump administration, arguably to test US strategy there – a classic 'know your enemy' approach – and Australia's strategy reflected this.

Second, the analysis tells us that, from a rhetorical perspective, US strategy focused on trade after the publication of its National Security Strategy (NSS), and the language used in association with trade became tighter. This can be explained purely in terms of game theory: the US approach is an individualistic one, centred around the assumption of its capacity to win. Its behaviour is rational, for it sees a conflict to gain power, whether trade, technological, economic, financial or military, as inherently winnable. It can therefore threaten and coerce without needing to take direct military action. The use of sanctions against North Korea, complicit with the UN and China, is evidence of what it was doing at the time. Its lack of military intervention in both North Korea and, in June 2019, Iran, despite provocation, suggests that there is indeed no appetite for military conflict: other weapons are being used, even if the desire to win is the same.

In short, we used to know the rules of the game, but these have become more complex in the multipolar and multidimensional modern world. What we do know is that we are witnessing a power play, and that winning seems non-negotiable at this point. Power is about coercion. Trade is the game, the weapon and the strategy. It is a proxy for a larger conflict, but its reach is big and the consequences of escalation and miscalculation where it is concerned are profound.

Financial 'boots on the ground'

Banking and finance are at the core of the power struggle, and it is impossible to ignore that. The financial system is, as ever, at the heart of the global economic system, and control of it, either nationally or globally, is a route to power. That is why trade is the focal point for escalation now. It creates a degree of national pride and, more importantly, marshals the financial system around one national objective: to promote the country's exports. We have said that using trade as a weapon of war is not a new idea. As it turns out, neither is using the financial system.

This has a practical effect. In the words of one senior banker: 'We are seeing an escalation of tensions against a general reluctance for governments to worry about the key things that might mitigate these tensions.' Such government involvement might include, for example, a clear focus on transparent and sustainable supply chains, avoiding environmental damage or know-your-client (KYC) and anti-money laundering (AML) violations. There is also an unwillingness to regulate the technology sector and its incursions into the financial space. What is happening, this banker felt, is the costs and responsibilities are being passed down to banks.

So, banks are operating in a new world where trade is weaponized and strategic. This matters because they are key actors in the trade system. Around US$9 trillion a year of the value of global trade is directly financed by banks through loans, letters of credit and structured finance, or by government-owned export credit agencies via guarantees, loans and insurances. Altogether, this is nearly 45% of world trade.

This number explains why banks need to worry about the political and economic risks inherent in trade, and why they should be concerned about the nationalist power play that is the main driver behind this trade war. Most critically of all, they need to understand the weapons that are being used. As the main financiers of trade, they are embroiled in conflict, whatever form it may take: sanctions or tariffs. The growth of banks' compliance functions over the past 10 years, for example, bears witness to the complexity of the regulatory, economic and risk environment that banks are facing. Banks are now part of the power struggle between nations as the latter adapt to the new paradigm; they are there by default.

In short, and as stated above, banks are a 'strategic tool, and a national security weapon'.[47] The trade finance sector is huge and there is a lot to lose, financially, reputationally and behaviourally. Unless banks can operate within the framework of sanctions, they will be fined. This undermines the work they have done since the financial crisis to safeguard the retail side of their businesses and, to quote one banker, 'make people love banks again'. This might seem like something of a tall order; and given the unpredictable and volatile sanctions environment, it is almost impossible.

Trade finance has had a tough time since the financial crisis. First, trade has failed to recover much beyond its pre-crisis levels in either value or volume terms. Despite the optimism for trade and the global economy during 2017 when oil prices started to recover, 2018 and the beginning of 2019 did not produce the trade growth either the WTO or the IMF expected. Combined with low yields and loose monetary policy, this has put a strain on the trade finance function remaining profitable.

Second, the compliance scandals that hit several global banks from 2012 onwards have led to a stronger focus on supply chain transparency. Estimates vary, but between the financial crisis and the end of 2018 approximately US$26 billion in fines for KYC, AML and sanctions breaches were imposed by global regulators.[48] At time of writing, over £300 million in fines has been imposed by the Financial Conduct Authority

(FCA) in the United Kingdom alone,[49] and that is excluding the US$947 million in fines to US authorities for irregularities in compliance reporting by Standard Chartered.[50]

Supply chains are becoming increasingly complex, both because of digital trade and because the components within value chains travel across borders many times before they are assembled into a final product. Knowing the details of a supply chain beyond where a product is sent is at best tricky and at worst undoable.

These cost and compliance pressures have triggered a move away from financing small and medium-sized enterprises (SMEs) towards supporting larger corporates. As a result, according to the Asian Development Bank, there is a US$1.5 trillion trade finance gap between the amount available to SMEs through banks and the amount SMEs actually need.[51]

This gap persists despite the increased number of financial technology (fintech) companies, and there is a very good reason why. The market is increasingly being developed by these companies and this has serious consequences: they are not banks and are therefore not regulated in the same way. Their supply chains are even harder to trace, and the scope for fraud or non-compliance within them is greater, because the links are becoming increasingly populated by the non-regulated fintech sector and not by regulated banks.

Finally, as if this were not enough, there is the backdrop of a trade war: the tit-for-tat escalation of the trade 'dispute' between China and the United States that has dominated the news since early 2018. The IMF claims that the tensions are affecting consumers and producers on both sides; but while there has clearly been some effect on trade between the two countries, the impact on economic growth, thus far, has been relatively modest.[52] In essence, what seems to be happening is that the tensions are fuelling anxieties regarding the perceived impact rather than the actual impact. To put it simply, markets rise when they think there is a deal in sight and fall when they think there is not.

Who wins?

Stock market growth has been a key measure of the US administration's successful implementation of its MAGA strategy. Thus far, although there has been higher volatility, market jitters have been contained and trade compared with a year ago was relatively robust to the end of 2018 (see figure 4).

Yet, there was a clear and visible drop in trade between October 2018 and February 2019, likely the result of tariffs being imposed between the United States and China in 2018. The former imposed US$250 billion in tariffs on imports from China during that year, and, as the IMF reports, this has reduced trade in the key affected areas: around half of US imports from China.

We do need to be clear on the size of this effect, because there is an element of seasonality to it: trade always falls between October and February each year, and it has done so by a global average of about 13% over the past five years. The US–China trade corridor appears to be particularly vulnerable to this seasonal drop: the average drop over these same months for the past five years has been 23% for US exports to China and 28% for US imports from China. The recorded drop of 7.6% in US exports to China between 2018 and 2019 is therefore low and may be explained by the Chinese stockpiling ahead of any future rise in tariffs. Meanwhile, US imports from China fell by over 36% during this time period, which is substantially higher than the five-year average. What is interesting, however, is that US exports to China have been on a downward trend since December 2017, and not just since the trade war became explicit policy accompanied by escalating actions.

December 2017 is a significant date for global trade policy, not because any particular measure or countermeasure was introduced but because that was the month the United States published its NSS.[53]

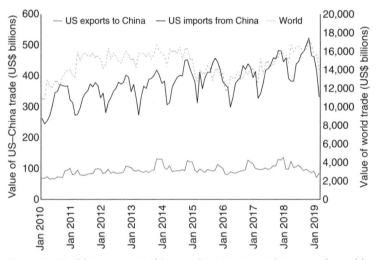

Figure 4. World versus US–China trade, imports and exports (monthly value, January 2010–February 2019, US$ billions). *Source:* IMF Direction of Trade Statistics, 2019.

The NSS was the first formal statement of a strategic shift in America's foreign and domestic policy, from its postwar 'global policeman' role to its MAGA agenda. Its publication marked the moment tariffs and sanctions became part of a strategy targeted not just at China but at US allies too. The strategy made it clear that 'the United States would no longer tolerate economic aggression and unfair trading practices'. [54]

From then on, a tariff could be justified on national security grounds. This cast aside the governing principle of the post-war General Agreement on Tariffs and Trade (GATT) that no nation would invoke national security in trade disputes because of the risk of retaliation. After all, if one country saw risk in the behaviours of another, what would prevent that other nation from staking the same claim? This is how the most recent game began. We are experiencing the power play right now.

Did anyone see the gorilla?

The use of game theory to understand what is going on with trade seems obvious: if country A imposes a tariff, how will country B retaliate? Will they impose an equal but opposite tariff? If they do, will country A impose another tariff, making country B escalate theirs? When will they stop? Who has the most power to keep going? Who will blink first?

This is a well-rehearsed scenario relating to the game of chicken in which we currently find ourselves. The United States has a trade deficit with China, Japan and the EU. This means that, theoretically, it can impose, or threaten to impose, more tariffs on imports coming into the country than its trading partners can impose on US exports. America wins because it is in the dominant position: as shown in figure 4, imports to the United States (in this case from China) fall because they are more expensive and consumers do not want to pay the higher price. Thus, the trade deficit falls, and a key policy target is met. This will be explored in more depth in chapter 4; what is important here is that this approach has been driven at an administrative level with the strategic target of reducing the US trade deficit.

Many economists would argue that reducing the trade deficit is both a red herring and misguided.[55] Quite apart from the fact that the US trade deficit has been growing since China came to power, they argue, closing the deficit is impossible. In a nutshell, the trade deficit contributes substantially to the indebtedness of the nation. American consumers buy a lot of goods and services and spend more than they earn. Unlike Germans, for example, whose country has the largest trade surplus in the world, Americans do not save. As a result, there is not enough money from savings in banks to cover the costs of investment. That money has to be borrowed: 70% from the Federal Reserve and US citizens, and the rest from another country that has a surplus. As a result, China owns about US$1.2 trillion of the United States' circa US$21 trillion debt; Japan owns over US$1 trillion of it and the eurozone owns over US$2.5 trillion of it. This is some 27% of the US$4.06 trillion in Treasury bills owned outside of the United States.[56]

It is not our purpose here to discuss the nature of the US deficit but rather to point out that this is a strategic weakness of the country. America is beholden to countries with whom it has a trade deficit. This is particularly true regarding China, who is not an ally and does not have a similar economic system. The very fact that China could topple the US economy by selling back its debt underscores this vulnerability. The US administration is therefore experiencing an existential crisis: how can a country with a different and competitive system of economic administration be not only a player in this strategic competition but also, more importantly, capable of winning it?

This focus on the US deficit makes a trade war inevitable. It is obvious in America's dealings with China in the first instance as well as with other surplus countries – especially Japan and the eurozone. The result, as stated earlier, is a pure and simple game of chicken.

Summing up

If something is being gamed, it is being used to create a strategic advantage somewhere else. To explain what is going on here, we need to look at the psychology of strategy. Strategy in this context is all about power and coercion. Competing powers will use different techniques or games to 'win', because winning is all about exerting your power or influence over the game. Essentially, in strategic terms, it *is* the winning and *not* the taking part that counts!

Power, whether hard or soft, is relevant in the approach a nation will take to playing a game. The softer the power, the more likely a country is to take a conciliatory approach: to want to bring actors together. Conversely, the harder the power, the more likely a country is to take a coercive line. This explains the apparently benign and multilateral – but, in reality, manipulative – game the Chinese seem to be playing as well as the equal but opposite coercive line of the United States.

This game cannot be expressed better than through a famous psychology experiment by Daniel J. Simons and Christopher F. Chabris in 1999 that illustrates inattentional blindness. Participants are asked to watch two teams of three pass a basketball to each other. Observers are asked to count the number of passes that three players wearing white shirts make. After about 30 seconds, a woman in a gorilla suit walks across the back of the court, faces the camera and thumps her chest. Focused as they are on the task at hand, just under half of the 192 observers (46%) watching the game miss the gorilla completely.[57]

At its core, strategy is a psychological exercise. By focusing the world's attention on trade, China and the United States have made us concentrate on what is visible: the perceived threat of an all-out trade war. Trade, the internet and finance are being weaponized, and this focus on trade is keeping us blind to the bigger picture: the fight to gain control of cyberspace. We think we are playing one game when we are actually being implicated in another, where the risks of escalation and miscalculation are higher.

Any strategy for action must construct a 'theory' of the current state of play: what does the world look like, where are the threats and how will others behave? As Colin S. Gray points out, strategy is adversarial, and a winning strategy is based on understanding the situation and how it is being played. Strategies are formed in times of peace and war, and they always seek control over enemies – and sometimes allies as well.[58] They contain theories about how to play the game: how to stake out positions and how to predict the behaviours of others. Theories, by definition, can change with the circumstances, even if the overall strategy remains the same.

As a result, we have also constructed a theory, effectively a scenario, so that we do not make the same mistakes in the future. We are watching a trade war evolve around us. But our theory here is that trade is the basketball game to the new paradigm's gorilla. Gaming trade means that it is being used to fight a separate, and much bigger, battle. If we can understand this, we can understand the behaviours at play and therefore the strategies to ameliorate those behaviours.

Chapter 3

The game plan

In the whole range of human activities, war most closely resembles a game of cards.

— *Carl von Clausewitz, 1832 (1976)*[59]

War and strategic trade

To look at why trade is being gamed in this way, and why
strategy is vital, we need to examine why the word 'war' is
appropriate in the context of trade. This chapter argues that,
historically, trade and politics have gone hand in hand, and
this means that, to a large extent, it has always been part of
the strategic 'game'. Here, we explore the theoretical link between trade and war and look more precisely at how game
theory helps us to understand the way in which strategies
are constructed, using examples from the current trade war
between the United States and China.

The obvious starting point is the Prussian general Carl von
Clausewitz's posthumously published masterpiece, *On War*,
one of the most widely quoted texts on the character and
nature of conflict. His statement that war is 'a continuation
of policy by other means' is still considered by scholars to be
the most precise definition of war and has been applied in

multiple contexts, ranging from *Politics by Other Means* by David Bromwich, which examines the 'collision of ideologies' in higher education, to `A marketer's guide to Clausewitz' by Bill Parks *et al.*[60] Clausewitzian purists will often recoil at such appropriations, but the use of Clausewitz's ideology across such a range of disciplines nearly 200 years after the publication of *On War* is a testament to the acuity of thought he demonstrated.

Indeed, our own analysis draws some parallels between the concept of trade war and conventional warfare as described by Clausewitz, i.e. that it must be violent, instrumental and political. All war *must* be violent; it is fundamentally 'an act of force', and although there is nothing inherently violent about trade, it can certainly be aggressive in character. Further, through the supply of arms and ammunition, trade can fuel conflicts: this renders it indirectly violent, or at least potentially motivated by violent intent. Further still, there is a wealth of historical evidence to suggest that trade wars often escalate into conventional military conflicts. Take, for example, the Opium Wars between the Qing dynasty and Great Britain (1839–1842 and 1856–1860), which saw a trade imbalance between the Chinese and the British escalate into a conflict that led to an estimated 20,000 deaths.[61]

In terms of the political nature of war, trade is also inexorably connected with politics. The concept of trade as an instrument of policy is often attributed to Albert O. Hirschman and his book *National Power and the Structure of Foreign Trade*, published in 1945. Using World War II as his case study, Hirschman wrote that 'relationships of dependence, of influence, and even of domination can arise out of trade relations'.[62] As Trump's use of tariffs clearly demonstrates, trade can be wielded coercively in order to bend other states to one's will. In addition, the pursuit of building one's own power while limiting that of others through coercing, integrating or building strategic potential by stockpiling goods heavily relies on trade. Suffice it to say that the political objectives of trade mean the overlap between trade war and conventional war is striking. Even Clausewitz wrote that trade and conflict have much in common, arguing: 'We could more accurately compare [war] to commerce, which is also a conflict of human interests and activities.'[63]

Arguably, there is no other point in time where this has been more the case than under Donald Trump's tenure as President of the United States. On 8 March 2018 Trump imposed 25% tariffs on steel imports and 10% tariffs on aluminium imports for all countries apart from Canada and Mexico, stating that a 'strong steel and aluminium industry are vital to our national security'. Trump faced tough criticism for the move, including from then Speaker of the United States House of Representatives Paul Ryan and former Secretary of Defence James Mattis, who both questioned the efficacy of the administration's approach. Specifically, they voiced concerns over an escalation of the trade war and the impact this might have on existing alliances. However, just a few days earlier (on 2 March), Trump had written on Twitter:

When a country (USA) is losing many billions of dollars on trade with virtually every country it does business with, trade wars are good, and easy to win. Example, when we are down $100 billion with a certain country and they get cute, don't trade anymore – we win big. It's easy![64]

In this tweet, Trump illustrates the zero-sum thinking that has characterized the United States' modern approach to trade, the construction of power and its quest for global influence. Trump's use of the terms 'win', 'win big', 'good' and 'easy' seems to illustrate a strategy derived from an interpretation of the basic minimax gains and losses tables found in game theory.[65] However, it should be noted that although the United States has been the most vocal and overt in how they have employed and deployed trade, they are not alone in their reconceptualization of the concept. There is also significant evidence that both Russia and China are using trade strategically in order to achieve a greater level of global influence. To paraphrase celebrated nuclear strategist Colin S. Gray, for the great powers, trade has increasingly become the means used by chosen ways in order to achieve desired political ends.[66]

Why has this occurred? In *The Art of War*, Baron de Jomini establishes 10 categories (or 'arts') of wars and explains how to wage them. It is his third category, 'wars of expediency', that is most interesting here:

> There are two kinds of wars of expediency: first[ly], where a powerful state undertakes to acquire natural boundaries for commercial and political reasons; secondly, to lessen the power of a dangerous rival or to prevent his aggrandizement.[67]

Of course, Jomini was not referring to the idea of a trade war in his analysis; he meant the use of conventional forces in order to build one's own power (political or commercial) while limiting that of one's adversary. The similarities between these and the objectives seemingly pursued by the Trump administration are nonetheless intriguing. The lack of a political will for direct military confrontation reflects our current reality, where nuclear weaponry has limited prospects for an all-out conflict between the world's great powers. States will now go to extreme lengths to wield the same level of global influence while avoiding conventional war. As B. H. Liddell Hart writes, nuclear weapons have fomented 'a reversion to the indirect methods that are the essence of strategy – since they endow warfare with intelligent properties that raise it above the brute application of force'.[68] These 'intelligent properties' include engagements in limited proxy wars, coercive diplomacy and, increasingly, the exploitation of the globalized economic system.[69] There is no guarantee that major war between great powers will not take place, however. As Herman Kahn argues, nuclear war may seem 'immoral, insane, hideous, or highly unlikely, but it is not impossible. To act intelligently, we must learn as much as we can about the risks.'[70] There will always be the potential for an escalation of tensions or the miscalculation of an adversary's intentions. Nevertheless, given the understandable reluctance for a war that would inevitably lead to mutual destruction, these great powers are seeking alternative means to increase their political strength through non-violent 'wars of expediency'. Within this context, trade becomes an attractive strategic option in the quest for global influence.

To be clear, we are not talking about the augmentation of state power simply by building a stronger economic base through mutually beneficial trade relationships; we are talking about what we term 'strategic trade', i.e. trade deployed in the pursuit of foreign policy objectives to gain a political advantage and to diminish the power or block the rise of a rival.

Strategic trade theory first emerged in the 1980s, with significant contributions from Barbara Spencer and James Brander in 1983 and 1985.[71] The term 'strategic trade' was first used by Paul Krugman in 1986.[72] Krugman correctly argued that trade is about more than just economics: it is politics, too. For Krugman, strategic trade was essentially protectionism. He suggested that governments could catalyse resource reallocation to the sectors and businesses where economic rents (i.e. returns to capital and labour) are highest, thus protecting them against foreign competition. He argued that trade was increasingly about taking national advantage of economies of scale and of the positive spillover effects (in simple terms, the positive unforeseen consequences) from technology and organizational learning.[73] However, our approach differs in that we see strategic trade as the use of trade to achieve foreign policy and even military objectives. This is strategy as it is often referred to in the international relations literature – or, as Michael Handel writes, as 'the development and use of all resources in peace and war in support of national policies to secure victory'.[74]

There are several ways that this can manifest itself. First – and most obviously, given the US–China trade war – is the application of trade as a tool of hard power. Hard power is usually seen as the use made of military force to compel an adversary to do one's will; however, it need only concern the attempt to coerce another actor (either a state or a non-state). Rather than using the carrot to influence others' behaviour, hard power uses the stick. We have seen multiple examples of this approach to trade since Donald Trump became president. China, according to Trump, is an 'enemy' of the United States and its only serious rival in terms of economic and military power.[75] His instigation of a trade conflict with China had all the hallmarks of Jomini's 'war of expediency': it served the purpose of gaining both political and commercial advantage by attempting to boost the value of US trade, protect US intellectual property rights and enhance US national security while simultaneously inhibiting China's influence and venturing to curb its rise.

Second, trade can be wielded as a tool of soft power. This entails bringing states closer through integration and mutual benefits in order to serve your strategic objective. To reverse our analogy above, this is using the carrot instead of the stick. China has favoured this strategy in recent years, which Xi Jinping refers to as 'soft power with Chinese characteristics', with the intention of becoming 'a global leader in national strength and international influence'.[76] Typically, this has entailed investment and infrastructure projects across Central Asia, the Gulf and sub-Saharan Africa as a result of China's BRI. In some ways, it is more effective than a coercive approach, as – due to the economic benefits it brings – this strategy makes other states more amenable to the growing level of Chinese influence. For example, Joseph S. Nye, the progenitor of the term 'soft power', wrote in 2005 that a BBC poll of 22 countries had found that almost half of the respondents viewed China as a positive influence; only 38% felt the same about the United States.[77] This was reaffirmed by a Pew poll in 2014, which found that sub-Saharan African states held overwhelmingly positive views of China.[78]

The third way in which trade can be deployed concerns neither hard nor soft power. It is an indirect approach that deals in the targeted supply of goods (either arms and ammunition or dual-use) to areas of the world deemed strategically important with the objective of (a) propping up local forces, such as militias, separatists and private contractors; (b) creating 'strategic potential' for the future by bolstering one's own military capabilities in a region; or (c) fuelling an allied state's military capabilities (e.g. through the provision of goods to develop a missile programme) in order to undermine the influence of a rival state or a collective defence alliance. This is the approach favoured by Russia, in part due to the fact that they cannot compete with either the United States or China on an economic level, but also because such an oblique approach to power-building tends to slip under the radar of most analysts and policymakers. As Hall Gardner writes, 'contrary to neo-liberal thinking, which argues that the process of globalization will lead to mutual trade benefits and less conflict, Russian concepts of non-linear warfare argue that global interconnectedness can be manipulated by states (and anti-state actors) to forcibly assert their own interests'.[79] In other words, Russia takes a more creative approach to trade, which transcends the traditional misconception that economic coercion through trade embargoes, tariffs or threats to oil and gas supply is the only strategic option. Thus, its interpretation of strategic trade is dominated by neither hard nor soft power; Russia's approach belongs to the realm of indirect or oblique power.

It is, of course, the case that each state will use a combination of all three measures outlined. As we illustrate in our case studies, China has often used trade coercively against the United States, Japan, the Philippines, South Korea and Taiwan.[80] Russia wielded trade as part of an integrative or interest-led strategy against Georgia prior to the outbreak of conflict in 2008; this strategy featured economic coercion as well as military tactics that would benefit Russian policy in the country.[81] Throughout its history, the United States has deployed trade via an indirect approach by propping up regimes and separatists through the provision of arms ammunition, perhaps most famously in 1986, when the Central Intelligence Agency began providing Afghan rebels with stinger missiles in their war with the Soviet Union.[82] The fundamental point, however, is that the United States, China and Russia are all using trade strategically and as a *de facto* substitute for conventional military means, the price of which, as Robert O. Keohane and Joseph S. Nye write, has become increasingly 'costly and uncertain'.[83] Trade has become the weapon of choice as each state pursues its own objectives.

Let the games begin

The overarching aims of the United States, China and Russia are broadly similar: the US national strategy states that the country intends to 'compete with all tools of national power to ensure that regions of the world are not dominated by one power'.[84] China's objective is to become 'a global leader … in international influence',[85] while Russia's national strategy from 2015 states that its aim is to 'consolidat[e] the Russian Federation's status as a leading world power'.[86] Despite this significant overlap, each of these states plays the game of power according to their own plan and their unique interpretation of the rules. What is clear in our current paradigm is that trade wars may become the new norm, so it will be helpful to comprehend the nexus between war and games as well as how we can use simulations to better understand the way trade is used in the modern era.

'Strategic theory is a theory for action', argues Bernard Brodie;[87] thus, theoretical discussions are only of use if they translate into practical solutions to a prevailing challenge. Therefore, the aim of the remainder of this book is to provide not only a theory of what we are seeing but also a strategy for action to build power and global influence. It may seem like an obvious point, but the fundamental reason for this is that the aim of any strategy is to achieve your objective (i.e. victory). Enhancing our understanding of the strategic trade phenomenon and how the great powers are deploying it is of paramount importance in achieving this. To quote the tagline from Donald Trump's ill-fated board game 'Trump: The Game', released in 1989: 'It's not whether you win or lose, it's whether you win!'

War, trade and games

For the purposes of this section, it is Clausewitz's observation on the similarities between war and cards (quoted at the start of this chapter) that provides our starting point. In fact, Clausewitz compares war to a game on several occasions; for example, he states that war is a 'duel on a larger scale' and encourages the reader to imagine a pair of wrestlers using both force (i.e. capabilities) and intellect (i.e. strategy) in order to overcome the enemy.[88] Clausewitz's point is astute: he is referring to the inherently adversarial nature of war (i.e. it involves two or more actors and necessarily results in a 'winner' and a 'loser').

This analogy also captures the dynamic nature of strategy insofar as one participant will attempt to execute their strategy at the same time their opponent tries to impose his or her own, while both attempt to block and counter each other's moves. Indeed, throughout history, games and conflict have held a very close relationship. The Chinese strategy game *Weiqi* (also known as *Go*), where players must try to capture more territory than their opponent, is thought to have been created 2,500 years ago by Chinese generals and tribal warlords, who would use the game to simulate upcoming battles.[89] Around the sixth century CE, the Gupta empire in India adopted the game *Chaturanga*. The name, which means 'four limbs' or 'four arms', refers to the four main units of the army: elephants, chariots, cavalry and infantry.[90] From here, strategy-based board games with a military connection grew in popularity across the globe, from *Shogi* (the 'Game of Generals') in Japan around the eleventh century CE, via *Shatranj* (four arms) in the Persian empire, to chess with the set of rules we recognize today from around the thirteenth century CE.

However, while the cerebral pursuit of chess and its non-Western equivalents were popular among the world's military elite for sharpening their ability to think strategically, games of this nature were not a true reflection of how to conduct warfare: if chess is pure, zero-sum conflict, real-life conflict is *more* non-zero sum. It was one of Clausewitz's contemporaries, Baron von Reisswitz, who solved this disjunction by developing the idea of a *Kriegsspiel* or war game. In 1824, his son, Georg Heinrich Rudolf Johann von Reisswitz, picked up this concept and published a set of rules.[91] To represent the battlefield, Reisswitz used accurate topographical maps with a scale of 1:8,000, which the Prussian army had just begun implementing, and chose painted wooden blocks to represent the units. The play was turn based, with commanders using real-life experience of warfare to govern their actions on the mock battlefield via statistics tables from actual combat, and dice rolls to determine a positive or negative outcome for each action as well as its level of effectiveness.[92] These rules injected the game with the crucial and immutable components of warfare that Clausewitz would later write about: chance, uncertainty and friction.[93] General Karl Freiherr von Müffling, Chief of the Prussian General Staff in Berlin and a specialist in military cartography, attended a demonstration of one of the *Kriegsspiele* and, recognizing its potential, allegedly exclaimed: 'This is not a game! This is training for war!'[94]

From this point on, simulating warfare has become the bedrock of most states' military strategy. In America, war games became common soon after the Civil War, and a number of Japan's victories over Russia in the Russo–Japanese war of 1905 were credited to the simulations that had been carried out beforehand.[95] However, it is perhaps the emergence of game theory, with the mathematician John von Neumann's 1928 article 'Zur Theorie der Gesellschaftsspiele' ('On a theory of parlour games') followed by Neumann and economist Oskar Morgenstern's seminal 1944 work *Theory of Games and Economic Behaviour*, that has had the most significant impact on conflict modelling. According to William Poundstone, 'game theory is the twentieth century's *Kreigspiel* [sic]' because it applies rigorous and complex mathematical concepts, assuming rational behaviour, to the field of human conflict.[96]

Of course, game theory began as an attempt to improve our understanding of economic behaviour. Like Clausewitz and his card analogy, Neumann and Morgenstern use poker (among other games) 'to find the mathematically complete principles which define "rational behaviour" for the participants in a social economy'[97] and to examine dynamic interactions and decision making in games between two or more players in order to uncover the optimum strategies that maximize profits and minimize losses. Ultimately, through a series of complex mathematical formulae, game theory's purpose was to provide a theory of 'marginal' or 'expected' utility in order to remove the element of uncertainty from decision making, taking into account variables such as random and mixed strategies, chance and the quality of information available to the participants of a game: for example, how the possession of 'perfect' or 'incomplete' information can affect decision making.[98] This point is crucial in understanding how strategies are formulated, given that the whole picture will rarely be available. However, perhaps the most widely known aspect of Neumann and Morgenstern's theory, and one to which they dedicate a significant amount of attention, is the concept of zero-sum and non-zero-sum games.

As previously stated, a zero-sum game is a mathematical representation of the situation where the gains of participant A are exactly equivalent to the losses of participant B, such that if the total losses are subtracted from the total gains they will equal zero. One of the most frequently used examples of a zero-sum game is the matching pennies scenario. This assumes two players are seated at a table and must simultaneously place their pennies down with either head or tails facing up. If the pennies match, then player A wins both coins. If they do not match, then player B receives them. According to Neumann's 1928 article, rationality is defined as an actor's attempt to minimize disutility while maximizing utility. Therefore, games of this nature are settled according to the minimax principle: as neither player has a limitation on payoffs, neither side is motivated to seek an alternative strategy (see table 1).[99]

Table 1. Illustration of a zero-sum game.

		PLAYER B	
		Heads	Tails
PLAYER A	Heads	+1 / −1	−1 / +1
	Tails	−1 / +1	+1 / −1

Conversely, a non-zero-sum game (also referred to as a mixed-motive game) concerns a situation whereby the aggregate gains of the participants can total more or less than zero. In such situations, players are faced with scenarios in which both can conceivably win and lose. Crucially, in non-zero-sum games, variables such as competition, cooperation and imperfect (or even no) knowledge of another player's intentions are factored into the equation, thereby removing the idea of 'pure conflict' that is a feature of zero-sum games. One classic example of a non-zero-sum game is the prisoner's dilemma, which was devised in 1950 by two RAND analysts – Merrill M. Flood and Melvin Dresher – who were working on game theory due to its possible application to US nuclear strategy.[100] The puzzle is this: two criminals are captured by the authorities and interrogated in separate prison cells. The authorities lack the evidence to convict them and therefore offer each prisoner the same deal: betray your associate and you will be set free while they get the maximum three-year sentence. There is, however, a catch: if the prisoners decide to betray one another, both will receive a two-year sentence; if the prisoners remain silent, both will receive a one-year sentence. The prisoners have no way of communicating and must therefore decide on their strategy to maximize utility while second-guessing the approach of their associate (see table 2).

Table 2. Non-zero sum games: the prisoner's dilemma.

		PRISONER B	
		Betray	Say nothing
PRISONER A	Betray	2 / 2	0 / 3
	Say nothing	3 / 0	1 / 1

It was games of the non-zero-sum variety that were of particular interest to celebrated economist and nuclear strategist

Thomas Schelling. He saw their potential military application, specifically in modelling optimum strategies for the nuclear stalemate between the superpowers – the United States and the Soviet Union – during the Cold War. In 1960, Schelling released *The Strategy of Conflict*, wherein he wrote that 'on the strategy of pure conflict – the zero-sum games – game theory has yielded important insight and advice'. However, he felt there was still much that could be added to non-zero-sum situations, such as 'wars and threats of war' and consideration towards the role played by 'suggestions and inferences, threats and promises'.[101] As a result, Schelling introduced his alternative matrix – with payoffs similar to those seen in the prisoner's dilemma – and applied this to three distinct situations being faced by the world powers at the time.[102]

1. *The nuclear arms race:* here, the assumption was that both sides would continue to augment their destructive capabilities. If both continued along that path, then MAD could ensue. If both agreed to limit their arms production, then both would win. However, if one side agreed to limit their nuclear arsenal and the other did not, then the former would be at a serious strategic disadvantage.
2. *A limited war:* here, the actors involved could gain an advantage by threatening to escalate the conflict – provided, of course, that their adversary decided to back down. If not, again, MAD would be the result. If this were a game of poker, this would be equivalent to going 'all in' with a weak hand and hoping your opponent did not call your bluff.
3. *Surprise attack:* this concerned the idea of an actor feeling threatened and carrying out the first strike against an adversary's nuclear arsenal. Schelling used the analogy of an armed burglar coming face-to-face with the also-armed

occupant of the house they are trying to rob, and raised the following, mind-boggling conundrum: 'there is danger that he [the burglar] may <u>think</u> I [the occupant] want to shoot, and shoot first. Worse, there is danger that he may think that <u>I</u> think <u>he</u> wants to shoot. Or he may think that <u>I</u> think <u>he</u> thinks <u>I</u> want to shoot. And so on.'[103] Worryingly, in this situation the least-worst option is to fire first. In his excellent and innovative book *Simulating War*, war game specialist Philip Sabin summarizes Schelling's three situations with the matrix shown in table 3.[104]

Table 3. Sabin's Cold War interpretation of Schelling's three-situation game.

	US stance is hawkish	US stance is restrained
Soviet stance is hawkish	Both sides lose	US loses, USSR wins
Soviet stance is restrained	US wins, USSR loses	Both sides win

Rationality and the role of culture

The problem with game theory is that it is a quantitative, mathematical expression of expected behaviour assuming participants will behave rationally. The Neumann–Morgenstern utility theorem argues that a player who is facing a situation in which they may lose must weigh up four conditions to maximize their gains: completeness, transitivity, continuity and independence. It classifies rational behaviour as a preference to maximize expected utility.[105]

This concept of rationality developed in the 1970s and is particularly important in the context of the current trade war. For example, mathematician Anatol Rapoport argued that at least two types of rationality emerge from the non-zero-sum model: individual and collective.[106] Using the matrix in table 3, individual rationality may rule that a hawkish stance is the more prudent course of action. However, in the context of global security, collective rationality dictates that restraint would provide the most mutually beneficial outcome. Of course, the latter approach is predicated on trust. If you are unable to trust your adversary's intentions, a hawkish stance becomes the most practical response again.

US political scientist Jack Snyder took this further by exploring the role of culture in determining responses to threats. Snyder coined the term 'strategic culture', which he defined as 'the sum total of ideas, conditioned emotional responses, and patterns of habitual behaviour that members of a national strategic community have acquired through instruction or imitation and share with each other with regard to nuclear strategy'.[107] He was concerned that the ethnocentrism of US analysts was leading them to erroneous conclusions; specifically, he was worried about the US conceptualization of a 'generic rational man' and how this person would use, or threaten to use, nuclear weapons. Snyder's point was that the Soviet idea of this man would differ significantly from the US view since 'individuals are socialized into a ... [distinct] mode of strategic thinking'.[108]

This was the so-called first generation[109] of strategic culture. The guiding principle of this version was that strategic culture is both the context that determines state behaviour and the 'constituent of that behaviour'.[110] Thus, strategic culture was considered to be 'modes of thought and action with respect to force, derive[d] from perception[s] of the national historical experience'.[111] It was perceived to be affected by geographical location, geopolitical environment, political outlook, military traditions and weaponry, bureaucratic institutions and the state of the relationship between the general population and the military.[112] Meanwhile, strategic behaviour was classed as actions taken 'relevant to the threat or use of force for political purposes'.[113] First-generation theorists argued that the Western strategic thinking of the day was dogged by ethnocentrism, and that the overarching influence of culture on behaviour guaranteed that a state's citizens and its institutions would be inexorably 'encultured'.[114] Therefore, strategists would 'continuously perceive and interpret the material realm culturally',[115] rather than according to the rational, utility-maximizing behaviour abstracted from game theory models.[116]

Ultimately, strategies are a function of their cultural and social contexts. As historian and political scientist Beatrice Heuser writes, 'the way a war is fought, and outside war, the way a strategy is formulated, is a function of the political system and the political culture from which they spring'; we are seeing this in the current power struggle as each of the big nations pits its own sense of history and manifest destiny against the rest.[117] Clausewitz teaches us that war is fundamentally a contest of wills; given that 'the will is itself a moral quantity' (i.e. culturally determined), it is these 'moral factors' that lend war both its nature and character. Further, they can alter and influence the objective of a strategy.[118] Thus, the significance of culture is ignored at the analyst's peril. Colin S. Gray opines that 'war, coercion and deterrence are all intercultural struggles' and, just as with Sun Tzu's famous maxim, it is essential to 'know your enemy'. After all, it is difficult to 'win' if you and your opponent are playing different games.

Same goals, different games?

US strategy is often referred to as a game of chess. In his book *The Future of Power*, Joseph Nye refers to the idea of power as a three-dimensional chessboard, with pure conflict taking place on three distinct levels. According to Nye, the first level concerns military power. Here, the United States reigns supreme and is unlikely to be overthrown by either Russia or China. The second level is economic power. Again, the United States dominates this, but the playing field has been levelled over the last decade; therefore, in economic terms, the world is far more multipolar. The third and final level relates to non-state actors. This includes bankers, hackers and terrorists: all the individuals and collectives that have an effect on global power distribution. At this level, no state holds central authority.

This idea of international relations, and particularly US strategy, echoing a game of chess was recently reiterated by Peter Navarro. While giving a keynote address at the EXIM Bank 2019 Annual Conference in Washington, DC, Navarro pledged to give 'a chessboard view of President Trump's winning economic strategies':[119] in other words, the strategy behind Trump's coercive approach to trade. In many ways, the comparison of US strategy to a game of chess is accurate. The pieces on the board include a knight, a castle, a king and a queen, and, as such, chess is intended to replicate a battle. The aim is to attack with military force from the start of the game, capturing (i.e. killing) as many of your opposition's pieces to inhibit their ability to counter your moves before declaring checkmate (from the Persian *shah mat,* which roughly translates to 'the king is dead'). This is emblematic of America's approach to foreign policy, which, according to William 'Trey' Braun, a retired US army colonel, usually strives 'to break glass, bring out the military and then go back to peace'.[120] Further, chess is a zero-sum game that is concerned with total victory for one participant and defeat for the other. As we argued earlier, much of Trump's approach is guided by the basic minimax principle, whereby the United States' gains are (in this case) China's losses.

This is not to denigrate the US approach: chess is an extremely complicated game. After each player has moved once, there are 400 possible moves. This increases to 197,742 following the second move and an incredible 121 million possibilities subsequent to the third. In other words, even a zero-sum game requires an incredibly sophisticated level of strategic thinking. We are making a general cultural point about US uneasiness with draws (or ties). For example, in 1954 a game of American football took place between Navy and Duke that ended with the scores at 0 – 0. When asked what it felt like, Navy's then coach Eddie Erdelatz responded with the infamous statement: 'It's like kissing your sister.' Our source for this quote states that '[n]o-one asked the mild spoken Navy coach to explain [what he meant]', although presumably he meant it did not feel quite right.[121] In 1974 the US National Football League (NFL) introduced the overtime rule to resolve any games that were tied at full time.

Much of the political rhetoric in the United States under Trump's tenure reflects this idea of winning. At a rally in Albany during his campaign for the presidency, Trump gave a passionate speech in which he stated:

> We're gonna start winning again. We're gonna win so much. We're gonna win at every level. We're gonna win economically. We're gonna win with the economy. We're gonna win with military. We're gonna win with healthcare and for our veterans.

We're gonna win with every single facet. We're gonna win so much, you may even get tired of winning!

Further, as Trump's chief economic advisor Larry Kudlow announced, 'most of all, I want America to win. I want America to win. And you [the EXIM Bank] can help us win'.

This rhetoric is also evident in the December 2017 iteration of the US NSS, which mentions winning five times. 'The future that we face is ours to win or lose,' it states. While discussing the nation's military capabilities, it explains: 'The size of our force matters. To deter conflict and, if deterrence fails, to win in war ...'.[122]

This contrasts starkly with the Chinese approach. If the US strategy is akin to chess, the Chinese strategy reflects the game of *Weiqi* (Go). *Weiqi*, which roughly translates to 'the game of encirclement', is often referred to as the world's most complicated board game. There are 10^{170} possible configurations of the board. According to Demis Hassabis, co-developer of the AlphaGo programme that managed to beat a human competitor at *Weiqi* for the first time, this is more combinations than there are atoms in the universe.[123] A typical board consists of a 19-by-19 grid. The players begin the game with 180 stones apiece, either black or white, and must alternately place them on the board at intersecting points. An opponent's pieces are taken by surrounding them with your own, and the game finishes when at least 50% of the board is controlled by one of the opponents and both players agree there are no more legal moves.

What sets *Weiqi* apart from chess is that there is no obvious military connection, and the primary goal is not to capture game pieces but territory. As the ancient Chinese proverb often quoted by Deng Xiaoping says, it is better to 'hide your brightness, [and] bide your time', building your forces slowly and steadily, and only revealing your strategy when it is too late for your adversary to counter it. The game begins with an empty board, meaning the information available to each player is incomplete. Further, there is no obligation to attack from the start, or even at all, with many games being resolved with very few stones being removed. The purpose is to win the game without overtly fighting, a philosophy that derives from the great Chinese general Sun Tzu, who wrote: 'For to win one hundred victories in one hundred battles is not the acme of skill. To subdue the enemy without fighting is the acme of skill.'[124] This is an acknowledgement that warfare can be psychological as well as physical and is vital to our understanding of strategy.

The parallels we have drawn here between chess, *Weiqi* and the respective strategies of the United States and China are clearly an oversimplification of reality. Nevertheless, these board games do reflect a certain mindset among the political elite of both the United States and China. This is largely due to the cultural point that the popularity of certain board games reflects the strategic preferences of a state. In the context of these strategy games, the respective approaches of the United States and China have been summed up perfectly by Henry Kissinger in his book *On China*: 'Where the Western tradition prized the decisive clash of forces emphasizing feats of heroism, the Chinese ideal stressed subtlety, indirection and the patient accumulation of relative advantage.'[125]

Tit-for-tat: tariffs

The question we must ask ourselves is this: how do these theories reflect the current reality in terms of Trump's trade war with China? In 1983, the film *WarGames* was released; it concerns a boy who unwittingly hacks into the US supercomputer (called Joshua) that controls the country's nuclear arsenal. Joshua believes it is playing a harmless game and is set to launch the missiles. In a last-gasp attempt to avert thermonuclear war, a team of scientists get Joshua to run through all possible scenarios that would lead to victory. After analysing thousands of situations, Joshua concludes with the following statement: 'A strange game. The only winning move is not to play.' Might we conclude the same for a trade war? As with an arms race, the only prudent course of action is to escalate or face a serious weakening of your position. It would be too much to ask to not escalate and hope your opponent follows suit. Further, standing up to a perceived aggressive action by an adversary is an essential part of any state's domestic strategy: no one wants to appear weak in front of their domestic support base. Therefore, the only option is to pursue an attritional strategy, continuing to match one's adversary's moves until someone capitulates or MAD ensues. In the meantime, in terms of the collective good, everyone loses. If we apply the possible outcomes to a game theory matrix, we can see that there is little hope (at time of writing) for a positive outcome if the trade war continues on its current trajectory (see table 4).

Table 4. Zero-sum game applied to the US–China trade conflict.

	US imposes tariffs	US does not escalate
China imposes tariffs	Both sides lose	US loses, China wins
China does not escalate	US wins, China loses	Both sides win

However, as previously stated, it is possible the United States and China are not playing the same game, and the erroneous assumption that comparable desired ends will lead to comparable means and ways being used could be undermining the ability of the United States to 'win'. The US administration could learn from the following anecdote. In 1980 Rapoport gave a series of lectures where he asked a simple question: what would happen if two individuals played out the prisoner's dilemma over and over again, knowing that they would be facing each other multiple times? In response to this question, political scientist Robert Axelrod set up a competition whereby game theory experts could enter a piece of code that would be pitted against other programmes in a round-robin fashion, with each game being played five times and comprising 200 moves. Rapoport's entry was called 'tit-for-tat', and, at just four lines of code, it was the shortest entry in the competition. His strategy was simple:

> Cooperate on move 1; Thereafter, do whatever the other player did the previous move.[126]

Incredibly, Rapoport's simple tit-for-tat entry won the tournament, beating programmes that had employed vastly more complex strategies. It was a good lesson for the other entrants, and, when Axelrod decided to run a second tournament, they were ready for it. Some of the new codes attempted to copy Rapoport's strategy before implementing a change at the last moment to win, e.g. the 'stab-in-the-back' programme would defect on the last round. The rules of Axelrod's second tournament were more complex than the first: he removed the limit of 200 moves and instead implemented a rule that gave a 0.00346 chance of ending the game with each move. There were 63 entrants in this competition, which meant over one million possible plays. Once again, Rapoport's tit-for-tat strategy won the tournament.[127] The crucial takeaway from this slight digression is this: Rapoport's programme penalized the opponent for self-interest and rewarded altruism. As soon as the opponent ceased to act according to self-interest, the reciprocal penalty was removed. In other words, tit-for-tat encouraged and rewarded cooperation. Returning to our modern example, the US instigation of a trade war has simply been matched 'tit-for-tat' by China. Both sides have the economic means to maintain their current strategy indefinitely, but neither side is likely to win. China is more than likely to remove its reciprocal tariffs if the United States chooses to do so first, but it will continue to be punished by China as long as it continues its current course of action.

The more pressing concern, however, is that there has been little consideration of whether China is using this tit-for-tat strategy in order to conceal or distract from its wider strategic aims. To continue with the chess analogy, the problem with the US administration is that all of its pieces are in plain view. Donald Trump has been very vocal not only about his intentions but also about what he wants Beijing to do. By contrast, as in *Weiqi*, it is very possible that China has not yet revealed its entire strength. The country's strategy is long term and characterized by, among other things, creeping territorial influence across the globe, stockpiling resources such as iron and steel and investing in ports in key strategic locations such as Gwadar in Pakistan. In other words, the binary 'I win, you lose' approach that has been adopted by the United States may harm its interests in the long run.

Chapter 4

The United States: coercion to win

Everyone likes to approach the challenges we are seeing now from different perspectives. Economists warn of the dangers a trade war will pose to global growth; commentators and strategists warn of a resurgent China, a lawless Russia and new wars in the Middle East; and lawyers point to US isolationism from the international treaties that have underpinned peace for the last 30 years.[128] As a result of all these different perspectives, it may seem that the neo-liberal agenda is 'irrational': for an economist, it makes no sense to embark on a trade war; for a strategist, it makes no sense to play the conflict game; and for a lawyer, it makes no sense to break the law. As we commented in the last chapter, it may be that the best – but also the highest risk – strategy is to shoot first.

To explain why the approach that the United States is taking at the moment is rational within its value system, we need to look at the picture as a whole, not as individual parts. US grand strategy has changed because the world has changed. In response to a more competitive, or 'weaponized', landscape, the United States has made trade the focal point of its foreign policy in order to restructure the world order in its own image.

As the US Export–Import Bank (EXIM) reported to Congress, the landscape of global trade has become 'weaponized'. The result is that the United States is at a competitive disadvantage, because trade, and the institutions around trade, have not hitherto been seen as 'strategic'.[129] In accordance with the country's MAGA rhetoric, reforming the WTO, redrawing the world's tariffs and focusing on homeland security through trade have all become priorities and are being addressed in 'Trump time': not over years but over weeks, and months only if necessary. For the rest of the world, this has been a jolt from the orthodoxy of globalization and convergence, and it has been palpable.

It is not even that Trump is seen to be wrong; in fact, in the quiet world of European export credit agencies, there is discrete acknowledgement that he is right. China has altered the rules of the game: money and tough non-trade barriers make it difficult to compete in our own backyards, let alone globally. It is simply that the US tactics of change have been brutal. In line with the neo-liberalism of the founding fathers of monetarism, its position is clear: America first and get used to it; play by our rules or not at all. This position is implacable, non-negotiable and direct. The fact that, slowly, the United States' partners are beginning to take a similar approach suggests that, underneath it all, there may be some truth to what is being said. It is just the *way* it is being said and the means being used to achieve it that are bothering the rest of the world.

Convergence? What convergence?

In a world where there are two military powers, each with guns and bombs pointed at the other, the rules of the game are simple. The game itself may not be as straightforward; after all, one power is trying to coerce the other into failure, and this requires complex strategy. Yet the objective is to win, and the rules are black and white: anything that builds power and makes the other look weaker is valid. The outcome is equally straightforward, because the guns and bombs are so powerful and the foreign policy reach of the countries is so great that winning is impossible, even though it is the purpose of the game. If one country fires a nuclear missile, the other will retaliate, and both will be destroyed.

The end of the Cold War and the subsequent era of 'convergence' ostensibly made strategy more complicated. If all countries are aligning around a shared set of economic and military interests associated with a rules-based liberal international order, then the greater good is multilateral rather than national. The nation state is subsumed into a network of supranational organizations, and there is no longer a need for foreign policy as such because when two countries do business together, they will not go to war.[130] Why, then, does the United States feel that the era of convergence is over and that the rules need to be recalibrated on its own terms?

The first reason, perhaps, is that the very concept of 'convergence' is a myth. US foreign policy after 1990 was driven by the country's desire to build and develop its 'military primacy'[131] as well as to promote its economic superiority by permitting nations previously seen as rivals to join its liberal system, so that they could benefit from America's technological, military, political and economic strength. The idea was that a 'unipolar' world with the United States at its centre would allow previously sworn 'enemies' to work together on shared issues such as climate change and economic development. 'Trade not aid' was a vital mantra of this era.

What America was effectively doing, though, was creating a global leadership succession plan. In the words of Thomas J. Wright, it was creating 'a global order that could survive the decline of the [United States]' through convergence.[132] The baton of power could pass seamlessly from the United States to, say, China, without any one country feeling worse off in terms of wealth or welfare. Each of the so-called Asian Tiger or BRICS nations now had the combined capacity to trump, so to speak, the United States' dominance, because (with the notable exception of Russia) they had growing economic power and, more importantly (in the case of China), an expanding trade surplus.[133]

Clearly, from a US perspective, this is not a sustainable foreign policy. The game has gone from one where, arguably, both sides could win against their value systems to one where the whole world may win but, ultimately, America will lose. Before the end of the Cold War, loss was unconscionable: to admit defeat meant a failure in military power. The existence of nuclear weapons made it possible to make a stalemate look like victory because each side could retain the moral high ground. The convergence era meant that foreign policy was subsumed into a greater multilateral 'good' and influence was exerted through the softest of powers: Cool Britannia, for example.

The second reason the United States is currently making waves is that convergence has led to an imbalance between America and its economic and military partners. Russia and China were, as has already been pointed out, very open to accepting US economic support while their economies were building, but they did not view the liberal international order as benign with regard to their own systems. Wright points out that Russia and China saw it as a direct threat: an attempt to 'democratize' them and 'deprive them of their sphere of influence'.[134] As early as 2007, when Putin broke with the United States at that year's Munich Security Conference, this convergence was showing signs of strain. In 2012, when Putin came back into power in Russia and Xi came into power in China, the cracks in the liberal order became very apparent. President Obama invested diplomatic effort into bringing China to the G20, but, as Wright argues, President Xi had inherited a China with vast military and economic capabilities, and 'as the first Chinese leader in 30 years not anointed by Deng, Xi was not bound by his formula'. In other words, Xi did not have to hide his brightness and bide his time; he could build his own mantra, 'Xi Jinping Thought', centred around the return of China to its natural place in history as a global power.[135]

Finally, the complexity of the security threat to the United States, and indeed the world, that convergence has unleashed was originally underestimated. Some non-state actors (e.g. terrorists or computer hackers) alongside smaller 'rogue' states such as North Korea and Iran have used the perceived threat of intellectual property theft to create a more complex security environment. For the US military, this has blurred the boundaries between conflict and civilian life. In the words of Rosa Brooks, 'all of our fine new technologies and fine new legal theories were blurring the boundaries of war, causing it to spread and ooze into everyday life'.[136] The game has changed, and the United States' new strategy is blurring the lines between the meaning of competition and the meaning of victory. For example, by declaring 'war' on a terrorist, the terrorist becomes a soldier and their cause is legitimized. In order to eliminate terrorism, then, that enemy and their cause must be 'defeated': this means strategy – and winning.

All of this combined after the financial crisis to catalyse the populism of which economic nationalism is the natural bedfellow. Presented with the results of convergence, citizens in the developed world and the emerging markets alike have felt the power of 'the other' outside of their control. This threatens their security and their economic well-being. In other words, the forces of liberal internationalism have given power to countries other than their own to control aspects of their lives over which they as individuals have no influence. Brexit in the United Kingdom and Trump's MAGA campaign are the outcomes of a collaborative game in which everyone, save the middle class/metropolitan elite, across the world appears to have lost.

Figure 5, which shows the trade surplus that the United States has with China for various activities in the service sector, gives us a clear indication of why the current administration feels there is a problem.

US service exports to China grew rapidly between 2011 and 2016. This was partly due to a low base value, but it also reflects the purchasing power of the Chinese economy as it integrated more into the global economic order. While annualized growth is projected to be significantly lower to 2021, it is still substantial.

This matters. The activities in the service sector are those via which intellectual property in the form of know-how and ideas transfers across borders. What is also remarkable about this chart is that five of the top ten sectors regarding US exports to China are directly related to intellectual property: government services (which is often military and educational); licences for the use of intellectual property; information services; research and development; and charges for the use of intellectual property. Paradoxically, the US service sector surplus could be accelerating intellectual property and knowledge transfer.

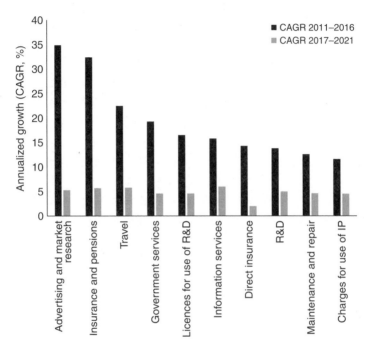

Figure 5. Top 10 service sector exports to China from the United States, 2011–2016 and 2017–2021 (projected), in Compound Annualized Growth Rate (CAGR) and percent (%). *Source:* Coriolis Technologies, 2019.

MAGA and the role of trade

Trump's key insight during his election campaign was that America's post-Cold War strategy had led to the country being cast adrift from its own 'God-given right' to liberties and freedom as well as its own founding values and beliefs, which have 'made the United States of America among the greatest forces for good in history'.[137] This sense of displacement, even uncertainty, about the role of US values in the world and at home was accentuated by the encroachment of products and services from abroad on American lives, because this seemed to supersede domestic policy to support jobs and livelihoods in 'old economy' sectors (e.g. agriculture, manufacturing, and iron and steel).

In essence, the MAGA campaign has as its founding principle the fact that if America looks after itself first, then it can look after others: 'A strong America is in the vital interests of not only the American people, but also those around the world who want to partner with the United States in pursuit of shared interests, values and aspirations.'[138] As Peter Navarro, Trump's trade advisor during his 2016 campaign, put it to an audience of banks and corporates: 'America first does not mean America alone.'[139] That is, by being strong itself, America is better placed to help other nations around the world.

This is an adapted version of the Cold War 'who blinks first' game, which opted for nuclear deterrence as an alternative to full-blown armed combat. The strategy is to build up the United States' political, military and economic strength and use its existing power – technologically and economically in the first instance – as a coercive tool for bringing other states into line.

The NSS could not be any clearer on why the United States has taken this stance: 'We stood by while other countries exploited the international institutions we helped to build. They subsidized their industries, forced technology transfers, and distorted markets. These and other actions challenged America's economic security.' It is equally clear that, for the United States, national security and economic security are one and the same. The NSS does not pull its punches when it states that, while it is not the intention to go to war, the United States will defend its interests economically and militarily.

What is interesting about the document, however, is that it is almost an economic policy document: it reads like an industrial rather than a national security strategy. This is the essence of the Trump administration's approach to the new competitive landscape. Four countries are named as security threats to the United States: China and Russia (the revisionist states), and North Korea and Iran (the rogue states). Yet it is towards China that the bulk of the measures in the NSS are really directed, because that nation embodies the systemic threat to America of intellectual property theft, cybersecurity risk, unfair trading practices, forced technology transfer, heavily subsidized state-owned enterprises, a deliberately weak currency and 'weaponized' overcapacity.[140]

The document is an explicit rejection of the convergence thinking of the Obama, Bush Jr and Clinton administrations. It argues that America can no longer think that integration into a US-led international order will make any of these foreign regimes benign. It justifies its policies on the basis that other states are catching up in terms of technology, their nuclear deterrence capabilities and their conventional military capacities. The NSS also highlights the risks of these states using data and information flows in order to gain power as being of even more concern, stressing that 'the ability to harness the power of data is fundamental to the continuing growth of America's economy prevailing against hostile ideologies and building and deploying the most effective military in the world'.

The cause of America's perceived weakness is crystal clear: as it supported international liberalism, it let its own military, economic, technological and political dominance weaken. Its new strategy, the NSS argues, is therefore to use 'all appropriate means' to further the administration's responsibilities of protecting people, safeguarding prosperity, preserving peace through strength and advancing US interests. To the extent that it is coercive, this strategy to strengthen US sovereignty will 'not impose, but will encourage cooperation with reciprocity'.

This boils down to three essential aspects of policy, which are used throughout the document to create direct actions supporting each of these 'responsibilities'. First, the administration will stop China's unfair trade practices – as well as those of others, including its allies – by using any tools it has at its disposal. It is evident from the NSS that the WTO system is regarded as unfair, and the United States is explicit in its desire to make some changes. In Trump's words: 'If they don't shape up, I would withdraw from the WTO.'[141] Similarly, it is clear that the United States regards its trade deficit with its competitors as the result of unfair practices which prevent US companies from exporting. Regarding China and US allies alike, the document states its strategic priorities as being to generate new trade and investment agreements, end foreign corruption, work with like-minded partners and promote the rules of a 'fair economic order' through competition and reform.

Trade – sanctions, tariffs and the rules of the trading system – alongside measures to protect data and information flows from cyberattacks and intellectual property theft are at the forefront of the NSS. They are also woven into the military and homeland security aspects of the document. The message is obvious: China's power has come about because it has been integrated into the global economic and intellectual property system, so it is this system that must be used to weaken Chinese power.

How does this translate into action?

The actions of the Trump administration have been largely conveyed to the public through the somewhat surprising medium of the president's Twitter account in the early hours of the morning. This means that an appearance of incoherence and confusion has pervaded the regime's strategic approach. In game theory terms, it might be argued that this plan of attack has been irrational: there is competition across a multitude of areas, particularly in relation to China, and this approach is seemingly so 'unstrategic' that it deepens the United States' risk of being sucked into a perpetual 'downward spiral' that cannot be stabilized.[142]

Yet there is nothing irrational or unstrategic about the way in which America is approaching the strategically competitive game it faces now. A review of the NSS above makes several things clear.

- Trade is the vehicle through which foreign policy and power is now being articulated. This is where the appearance of unfairness is most obvious to the public eye and therefore the way in which the politics of rebalancing the world's power relations can be most readily articulated.
- The weapons for fighting a trade war are simple and well documented. They are rhetorical and literal: belligerent language that increases tensions and tariffs as well as sanctions that do minimal damage to the US pursuit of economic growth and wealth, but which affect the way in which other countries operate.
- Military strategy is in a support position and is viewed as providing the contingency for dealing with rogue states and protecting US homeland security. President Trump

himself, and the NSS along with him, has made it clear that the United States will 'protect its interests' but will not deliberately seek war.

- Data – and control of the intellectual property and cyber-space through which data and information flows, is accumulated and is controlled – is key to ensuring the United States retains its global leadership role.

America must defend itself, so whether its relationship with China *can* be stabilized is the wrong question. The question should be this: why *has* the US–China relationship stabilized? Even if it may not look like it from the outside, the current stand-off, or fragile equilibrium, between the two is indeed a stabilization.

The reasoning behind this is as follows: the United States has raised the stakes, having imposed 25% tariff rates on US$200 billion of Chinese imports at time of writing. China has retaliated insofar as it can, with tariffs on US$110 billion of US exports to China. The United States can raise tariffs on a further US$325 billion of Chinese imports, but beyond that escalation is likely to go into the realms of non-tariff barriers, such as barriers to doing business with Chinese technology companies or a 'blacklist' of US companies along with hidden regulatory hurdles or even sanctions. The United States knows that China has a lot of cards to play in this space and has tried to seek a first-mover advantage by alerting its allies and US corporates to the security risks of working with Chinese interests in 5G networks. It has accused Huawei of sanctions breaches in Iran. It has prevented its own technology companies from working with Chinese firms that represent a potential security threat. China has drawn up its own blacklist of American businesses as a result and, more significantly for US energy interests, has imposed tariffs on imports of US liquefied natural gas (LNG).

This is key because China is a major consumer of LNG, so it seems perverse for this country to impose tariffs here since it has set great store by using LNG as an alternative energy source, thereby staking its claim to a more environmentally friendly energy policy. Figure 6 shows that the United States is actually China's fifth-largest LNG source, and although it is an important route for America and has been growing annually as a proportion of all Chinese LNG, it has not grown as quickly or substantially as Chinese imports from Australia, for example.

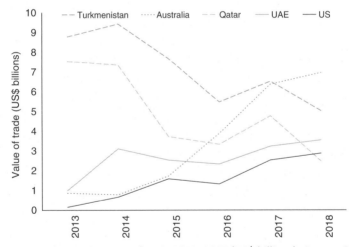

Figure 6. Chinese imports of LNG, 2013–2017 (US$ billions). *Source:* Coriolis Technologies, 2019.

US trade representative Robert Lighthizer has been clear that trade negotiations are complex and getting them right is vital to America's long-term interests. This is the case for all negotiations, not just those with China; but China is the benchmark because it is the core strategic competitor identified in the NSS. It is the test case for redrawing WTO rules because it embodies the 'non-reciprocal nature of trade that is harming this country'.[143] The task is to find a structure that will endure legally as well as politically. The fact that talks stalled in May 2019 was an indication that this tit-for-tat trade arms race would get dangerous if left unchecked. Trade has become a deterrent to a bigger set of financial and technological actions in the absence of any scope to use military means.

What has become clear in the period since the NSS was first published is the explicit way in which the United States is suspending the WTO's ability to act in a dispute resolution capacity. Trade disputes are heard by up to seven appellate judges. However, their appointment and reappointment must be approved by all members of the WTO, and America has been blocking each one as their terms have expired. This means there are now only three judges left and, as two are set to retire at the end of 2019, the dispute system will grind to a halt. This is strategic too: the United States is using the appointment system as a way of triggering reform at the WTO with regard to intellectual property theft and digital trade.

It is worth dwelling for a moment on the role that China has played in redefining America's relationship with the world order and the WTO in particular. One of the reasons why China and the United States reached a stalemate during their negotiations in May was because China insisted on reciprocal dispute resolution systems. The United States argued that, given China's lack of transparency, it could not guarantee that China would carry on the terms of any agreement 'in good faith', and therefore some right of appeal was necessary. China accepted this on principle but argued that there had to be a reciprocal enforcement arrangement.

This is interesting because any enforcement mechanism would have been directly associated with the key areas of interest in US–China negotiations: the trade balance, the purchase of US agriculture and manufactured products, the intellectual property regime, financial access to markets, cybersecurity and currency manipulation. Agreements around these would have been formed on a bilateral basis without any need for the WTO. It is quite clear why China would want these to be bilateral: it makes sure China's position as the largest trading nation in the world is acknowledged and that its stance is a simple statement of equal but opposite power. However, it is less clear why the United States might accept this from China.

Nevertheless, in agreeing to a bilateral enforcement mechanism outside of the WTO, America is further undermining the WTO's position and thereby putting further pressure on it to reform. The only issue is that, for both sides, a non-WTO agreement is not enforceable and is therefore inherently unstable. This is the essence of the challenge that those undertaking discussions are facing.

Negotiations with other parts of the world are in the same holding position. America's negotiating stances towards Japan, the EU, the United Kingdom and the NAFTA countries are all identical in mood and format, focusing on identical areas:[144] the trade deficit, US agriculture and manufacturing, intellectual property and cybersecurity, access to markets (especially the procurement of government contracts) and currency manipulation. US strategy is to influence its allies: not only in trade and digital space, or in terms of how they work with frontier technologies such as 5G, but with regard to monetary policy as well (since interest rate decisions affect currency values, at least in the short term).

US trade with its allies is no less strategic and no less coercive. In game theory terms, the United States is trying to influence the behaviours not only of its adversaries but also of its partners. The NSS makes it clear that America will work with 'like-minded' partners on its terms. The negotiations to create a new US–Canada–Mexico Agreement (USCMA) and to come to similar agreements with the EU and Japan are simply a statement of power. The United States is not willing to play everyone else's convergence game anymore. It has defined its own game with its own rules; if anyone wants to take part, they must play by these rules and not those that dominated the post-Cold War era.

There are two other areas where trade is being used to achieve non-trade strategic goals. First, the NSS is clear that the so-called rogue states (Iran and North Korea) are dangerous and need to be brought under control. The issue of North Korea's nuclear tests is the most straightforward: China accounts for some 85% of North Korea's trade, and it is clear when dual-use goods have trickled across the border (see figure 7).

The period shown in this figure is the era associated with convergence and liberal internationalism. It shows that North Korea received nuclear-related materials the year before its second nuclear test on 25 May 2009. In addition to this, in spite of agreeing to halt its long-range missile tests in 2012, the data shows increases in imports from dual-use sectors related to aerospace and propulsion equipment. While there is no evidence of where these trade flows came from, the conclusion is simple: trade has enabled an otherwise reclusive state to access materials which have allowed it to enhance its nuclear programme.

China becomes an obvious target, and early discussions between this country and the United States focused on dealing with North Korea as a common problem: an unpredictable ally in China's case and a nuclear threat in America's. North Korea became a proxy in early jousting matches between China and the United States, and the former's adherence to tough sanctions imposed by the UN meant that it could be seen as toeing an international but US-led line.

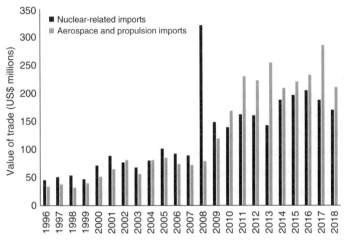

Figure 7. Dual-use goods flows between North Korea and the world (nuclear-related, and aerospace and propulsion), 1996–2016. *Source:* R. Harding and J. Harding (2017).[145]

It is not our purpose to discuss the effectiveness of this strategy. However, it is interesting that North Korea, in its desire to be taken seriously, provoked the United States until presidential summits were held. The resultant stalemate may well turn into a long-term solution while another recalibration of the global system takes place.

Iran also falls into this category. In 2018 the United States withdrew from the 2015 Joint Comprehensive Plan of Action to limit Iran's nuclear capability, nominally because of Iran's status as a 'rogue state', not to be trusted due to its links with terrorist groups, and because of its perceived failure to comply with the terms of the deal. A series of US-led sanctions has followed since then, limiting trade both with Iran and with individuals associated with Iran, its networks and its nuclear interests.

The heavy use of sanctions has created severe economic hardship for the Iranian economy and made the world trade system substantially more complicated from a financial point of view. Any trade deals that are priced in US dollars have effectively been closed off because the United States will not trade with Iran, and sanctions against individuals and institutions have created a complex, ever-changing web of compliance complexities for banks and businesses looking to work in Iran. The target is arguably not just Iran's regime and the 'individual threats' it may pose; it is the oil the country produces as well. This is the case for two reasons. First, after lifting a 40-year ban on oil exports in 2016, the United States has become a net oil exporter. Second, the Straits of Hormuz are vital to global oil trade. Some 21 million barrels of oil a day go through this route, representing nearly one-fifth of the world's oil production.[146]

The effect of this on the world trade system is twofold: it increases the complexity of the compliance function in global banks, and it puts further coercive pressure on allies to conform with US strategy. This latter point is important because it has created a push by European businesses for alternative structures to allow them to continue to trade. The Instrument in Support of Trade Exchanges (INSTEX), for example, is a special-purpose vehicle supported by the United Kingdom, Germany and France that allows businesses wanting to trade with Iran to access finance. We will return to this in subsequent chapters, but what is interesting here is the businesses that may have decided to use this vehicle, as well as the financial messaging system SWIFT, have decided not to trade with Iran for fear of regulatory backlash from the United States.

Iran has not been brought into line, however, despite the fact that it continues to provoke the United States. This shows the relative unimportance of US military strategy compared with trade strategy in foreign policy, as well as America's desire to redraw the world's trade lines. In June 2019 Iran shot down a US drone in its airspace. Despite an increased US military presence in the region and suggestions that there would be military repercussions, President Trump withdrew from a planned airstrike at the last minute, stating that it was not a proportionate response because of the number of casualties that would be incurred.

Given America's military strategy elsewhere in the Middle East, is Iran simply another vehicle for a US recalibration of the global supranational organizations that have governed trade and foreign policy in the post-Cold War era? By acting as it has towards Iran, the United States has done several things: it has legitimized Israel's dealings with Syria, it has taken an approach to foreign policy different from that agreed multilaterally at a UN level and, by using sanctions, it has forced its allies to fall in line if they want to avoid huge non-compliance fines. America has also made sure that all financial messaging and transactions flows remain focused around US interests: in other words, it retains US-dollar hegemony in the digital trade world. The United States, as is clear in its NSS, does not want to go to war militarily – but that does not mean it will avoid conflict if the objective is to rebalance the rules of trade in its favour.

There is a further area of US policy that is closer to homeland security but is equally being tackled through trade. The

United States has a budget deficit with the NAFTA countries and regards Mexico's rise as particularly problematic because it has competed in traditional rust-belt areas of intermediate manufactured goods, e.g. car components, electronic components, machinery and equipment. In effect, Mexico has become America's new China: a large amount of supply chain production has been taken away from the latter and relocated to the NAFTA region.

America's negotiating stance with these NAFTA countries is emblematic of its position on agriculture and manufacturing jobs, and involves speaking directly to its domestic audience. The current administration has stated that jobs have been lost to Mexico – particularly since 1994, when NAFTA was established – not least because many of these jobs were created on significantly lower wages than could be paid in the United States. The result for America has been a loss of economic power because of its reliance on workers in Mexico. Canada has not been an innocent bystander, either: higher tariffs were being imposed on US agricultural products than the United States was imposing on equivalent imports. Addressing this was a central pledge of Trump's election campaign.

The USCMA is, at time of writing, still waiting for Congressional approval. However, its key elements cover the rules of origin issues associated with US automotive supply chains across the region; worker rights and salaries to prevent Mexican workers from being paid less; and pledges to improve North American agricultural trade by making it fairer. It also includes provisions for intellectual property and procurement that will ensure US companies in particular can compete in both Mexico and Canada.[147]

What it does *not* deal with is the NSS's core concern: border security. This was addressed in June 2019 with a threat to impose tariffs on Mexican goods, starting at 5% and increasing to 25% if Mexico did not come to an agreement with the United States on the number of migrants crossing the border into America.[148] Mexico expressed its willingness to come to a deal almost immediately, but this represented a major shift in the use of tariffs for coercive homeland security reasons.

The only surprise is that any of this is remarkable. The US NSS was published in 2017. It does exactly what a strategy document should do: identifies risks, addresses gaps and puts actions in place to mitigate risks and build interests. What it makes abundantly clear is that trade is the modern foreign policy weapon of choice for recalibrating institutions, structures and assumptions of post-Cold War liberal internationalism. Every region is met with a negotiating stance that starts with brinkmanship, moves to coercion and ends with an arrangement that can be represented as a 'victory' of America first values. This is the zero-sum approach to strategy we referred to in chapter 3, whereby China's losses are America's gains. Below, we include table 4 again to illustrate this theory.

	US imposes tariffs	US does not escalate
China imposes tariffs	Both sides lose	US loses, China wins
China does not escalate	US wins, China loses	Both sides win

Chapter 5

China: the long game

Since becoming General Secretary of the Communist Party of China (CPC), Xi Jinping has placed his country at the centre of the world stage. His political ideology of 'socialism with Chinese characteristics' uniquely combines the long and rich history of China as a trading nation with its future desire to be the standard bearer of globalization and an open world trading system. Xi's goal is to restore China to its former glory. Such a policy also includes championing the environment and sustainability, bringing the Chinese model of economic growth to parts of the globe that have hitherto been unable to engage in the world trade system and, most importantly, increasing China's self-sufficiency in manufacturing as well as digital and artificial intelligence-based technologies. The game, if there is one, is not to 'win' in the same way that is meant by the United States but to gain influence for this Chinese model.

Xi's 'thoughts' on socialism with Chinese characteristics have been enshrined in the Chinese constitution since 2017, and in 2018 the rules governing succession to top Chinese posts were removed. In George Magnus's words, this makes President Xi 'a dictator with more personal authority than anyone since Mao Zedong'.[149] His standing and thinking have been pitched to a world that has seemed leaderless and without a clear definition of what 'liberal international order' actually means since the financial crisis. Against a global back-drop of lacklustre economic growth and a collective capitalist identity crisis, China's growth has seemed extraordinary. It now presents a competitive threat to the West because it jeopardizes particularly US hegemony in the financial mar-kets, the digital economy, technology, and – perhaps most importantly, from a legitimacy perspective – manufacturing and trade.

China's strategic challenges are, arguably, slightly differ-ent to the other case studies in this book. China has become a powerful nation because of its long history of reform, not just because of its integration into the liberal economic order after it joined the WTO in the early 2000s. As Magnus puts it, CPC officials argue that China 'stood up' under Mao, 'got rich' under Deng and 'became powerful' under Xi.[150]

However, this summary hides a lot of the complexity within China that forms the structure of its foreign and eco-nomic policy now. China faces not only the challenges of envi-ronmental degradation and sustainability, writ large through considerable pollution in its major cities, but also those of any emerging economy. Its average GDP per capita is US$8,000 annually (America's is US$56,000),[151] so while we talk of the threat of China's technological dominance and its aspirations to be a manufacturing super power, we must remember that it does not yet have the level of wealth required to qualify for the OECD, for example. To paraphrase Anjani Trivedi: China may well modify its growth targets, but while it will not rein in its power-related objectives, it is a long way from achieving them.[152]

China's biggest challenges are centred around this dichotomy: its status as a global power conflicts directly with its status as an emerging economy. Xi is currently one of the most powerful men on Earth, exercising tight control over his party, which he guaranteed through a clampdown on corruption in the early days of his leadership. He does not hold the view that Hong Kong or Taiwan should be outside of Chinese governance; this creates the potential for non-stop conflict, as we saw with violent protests in Hong Kong throughout the summer of 2019. The tense relationships between Hong Kong/Taiwan and China are at the heart of the latter's trust relationship with the rest of the world. China believes that the 'motherland' should have primacy over everything, and that both Hong Kong and Taiwan are part of this motherland. Any interference from outside (e.g. from the British in Hong Kong or from the Americans in Taiwan) is seen as hostile.

Domestic foreign policy?

China's international relations are not transparent. If there is a foreign policy game afoot, it is not easy to see how it is being played – or, indeed, who is playing it. There is, however, a lot of commentary on the 'assertiveness' and even the 'aggression' of China's foreign policy, particularly since 2010.[153] Xi's ascent to leadership has been accompanied by more direct statements of power. His 2017 speech to the 19th National Congress of the CPC, for example, claimed that China was a 'mighty force' in international affairs. It went on to state that the military 'must regard combat capability as the criterion to meet in all its work, and focus on how to win when it is called on'.[154]

This statement was taken by outsiders to mean that China was combat ready. The expansion of its military spending has reinforced this perception: China is now the second-biggest buyer of military equipment in the world.[155] The country has built islands in the South China Sea and has engaged directly with Japan, sending patrol ships and fighter jets to the Diaoyu/Senkaku Islands after Japan bought them in 2012. Both countries claimed historical rights to these islands, and while their conflict did not culminate in a clash of militaries, it did lead to a significant reduction in trade between the two countries for a period of two years.[156]

China's foreign policy is predominantly focused around its economic interests, and while this policy has certainly become noisier, in essence it still subscribes to the same five principles that were set out in 1954 by then premier Zhou Enlai. These are: mutual respect for each other's integrity and sovereignty; mutual non-aggression; mutual non-interference in each other's affairs; equality and cooperation for mutual benefit; and peaceful coexistence. As such, they are like the Marxist–Leninist principles of peaceful coexistence identified by Nikita Khrushchev,[157] but with three important differences: first, China's foreign policy includes an adherence to free trade; second, it prioritizes national sovereignty; and third, it excludes Taiwan from its definition of coexistence.

It is this focus on trade and nationalism that is the essence of Chinese foreign policy. Its current strategies, which include Chinese growth and economic development, are designed to promote the well-being of Chinese citizens. While their language may have become more aggressive, Xi's strategies – Made in China 2025 and the BRI – are simply addressing strategic threats as China sees them, and, in the case of the BRI, putting the country back at the centre of global power where it belongs. This is the crux of the problem in terms of how the West perceives China. As Henry Kissinger said in a 2018 interview, the United States and China have some strong similarities: 'We are two countries that believe they have an exceptional nature in the conduct of policy: we [the United States] on the basis of the political system of democratic constitutionalism; China on the basis of an evolution that goes back at least to Confucius and centuries of unique practice.'[158]

In this sense, China is playing ancient games of economic influence rather than exerting military power. Its foreign and domestic policies are indistinguishable, and – in the current climate of paradigm shifts and transition – easy to misinterpret.

The strategy

Magnus[159] identifies four strategic threats or 'traps' that China is facing: debt, an ageing population, the undetermined role of the renminbi and its status as a middle-income economy. He adds that China also has a trust problem, and it is perhaps this that, at present, is the biggest threat to its exponential development since the financial crisis.

There are three areas where this trust issue is most severe. The first is in China's dominant industrial policy: Made in China 2025. This was built on the Japanese and German industrial policies (Industrie 4.0) and is designed to promote China as it moves from being the world's 'factory' to a country that is on the leading edge of independent innovation and manufacturing as well as intellectual property development and sustainability. The second is in the BRI. This is a plan to expand the Chinese trade model along the routes of the old Silk Road, with substantial investment in ports and maritime capabilities as well as infrastructure through Eurasia to Russia and the Middle East. The third and final area is in Chinese claims to the South China Sea, which conflict with not only the interests of many Association of Southeast Asian Nations (ASEAN) countries but also with the interests of Japan, Australia and the United States in this region.

This chapter looks at each of these areas as case studies. Throughout our analysis, it is important to remember one point. Under Deng, the mantra for policy was 'hide your brightness, bide your time'. In other words, if you are strong, there is no need to make a noise about it. Xi has identified in US belligerence some scope for a more explicit statement of Chinese ambitions across these three areas. While China does have a debt problem – in 2018 its debt was some US$5.2 trillion, or nearly 48% of Chinese GDP – the question remains: does this debt represent a fatal blow to the Chinese model, because it will mean the country must rein in its ambitions, or has it been a trigger for the more direct approach to global reach that the Xi administration is now taking?

Made in China 2025

Made in China 2025 is not the first industrial strategy of postwar China, but it is the most ambitious. It addresses the four traps Magnus pinpointed by putting into place a strategy to achieve the following.

- Create an innovation-driven manufacturing base focused on quality and sustainability at the high-skill end of the value chain.
- Improve Chinese industry's productivity and performance, and invest in technologies that will allow it to compete at

the top of the global value chain. The goal is to make Chinese manufacturing independent by 2025, moving from 40% local content to 70% local content in the intervening years.

- Use state funding to promote an overall framework for the independent development of intellectual property through an effective fiscal and financial regime to support high-end innovation, particularly in big data and artificial intelligence.
- Develop a framework for allowing SMEs to work more independently, including by allowing them to develop their own intellectual property standards independently of the state.
- Allow businesses and financial institutions to invest in overseas businesses.

A total of 10 key sectors are promoted within the Made in China 2025 framework: advanced IT, automation and robotics, aerospace, maritime and high-tech shipping, modern rail transport, new energy vehicles, power equipment, agricultural equipment, new materials, and biopharmaceuticals and medicine. Some of these sectors overlap, but the growth in Chinese imports and exports since 2012 in the broadest eight categories can be found in figures 8a and 8b.

These are strategic sectors, with a high proportion of dual-use goods, but the figures make for interesting viewing. They are also the largest trading sectors for China (with the notable exception of arms and ammunition, which relates only to small arms and not to bigger military infrastructure). China's exports of ships and boats have grown at an annualized rate of over 18% since 2012; this figure is nearly 5% for transport equipment and pharmaceuticals, and over 4% for machinery and components, which includes electronic hardware. Imports of aerospace, arms and pharmaceuticals have all grown and while these did not grow in the 2012–2017 period, they are projected to grow in the future, reflecting their emphasis in the BRI project perhaps.

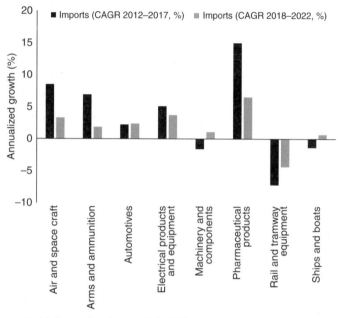

Figure 8. (a) Annualized growth in BRI strategic sector imports, 2012–2017 and 2018–2022 compared. *Source:* Coriolis Technologies, 2019.

This tells us several things about the Made in China 2025 strategy. First, it shows us that there is some self-sufficiency in the infrastructure of trade. This is especially true of transport and electronic infrastructure, since exports are growing more quickly than imports in those areas. However, it appears that in pharmaceuticals and aerospace exports are growing less quickly than imports. China has a trade deficit of US$17 billion in pharmaceuticals and of nearly US$22 billion in aerospace. This suggests that China has a long way to go before it becomes dominant in these sectors.

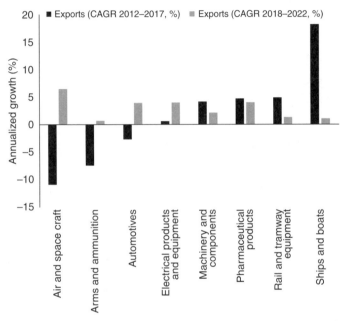

Figure 8. (b) Annualized growth in BRI strategic sector exports, 2012–2017 and 2018–2022 compared. *Source:* Coriolis Technologies, 2019.

So, the overall profile of trade in China is still that of an emerging economy. It has surpluses in lower-end manufacturing (e.g. clothing and toys) and intermediate manufacturing (e.g. electronics and electrical equipment). The country has more going on at the higher end of the value chain than it did, say, 10 years ago, but the whole purpose of this strategy is to put China on track to grow its capabilities in areas that modern developed economies are already operating in.

The important point is this: the Chinese economic model permits reliance on state support, while the liberal free market model does not. The sheer scale of investment and outreach attached to Made in China 2025 has rendered the country a strategic competitor economically with the United States. No one knows precisely how much is invested in this programme, but it is thought to run into the 'gunsillions'.[160] China's social-ism with Chinese characteristics model, combined with the power that Xi wields, may explain why this strategy is so easy to misconstrue.

Belt and Road Initiative

Analysis of the BRI has changed since it was first announced in 2013. Initially, it was seen as an opportunity for global businesses and finance to invest alongside Chinese financial interests and create a trade route that would bring eco-nomic development and prosperity to the region. More re-cently, the initiative has seen accusations of being a means for China to extend its power and influence, even though – as we can see from the analysis of foreign policy above – the country is only protecting its domestic interests, including its energy security. It is, in essence, a domestic policy: China is not simply exporting its trade surplus; it also has stock-piles of cement, iron and steel that it can use to, in its words, further the economic development, peace and prosperity of other nations.

Since 2013 China has had ambitious plans to build trade infrastructure and connections through Eurasia and into Europe as well as to enhance its marine presence by sub-stantial investments in ports across East Asia. Since China's economic policy is also its foreign policy, this seems like a plan to extend its influence upwards and outwards, through Kazakhstan, Mongolia, Russia and Iran, although the country's policymakers regard this plan as peaceful and aimed at fuelling economic prosperity in these and other nations in the region. China's goal is to convey the benefits of development through trade that it has experienced to other nations by facilitating infrastructure investments along what was known as the Silk Road some 2,000 years ago.

For this reason, McKinsey & Company likens the project, if successful, to a twenty-first century Marshall Plan that could amount to an annual infrastructure expenditure across Eurasia, East Asia and the Middle East to the tune of US$2–3 billion. The reach covers some 65% of the world's population, one-third of the world's GDP and over a quarter of all cross-border goods and services trade.[161] The so-called belt is a railway from Asia to Scandinavia, while the road, somewhat confusingly, is the old maritime Silk Road that covers the ports and shipping lanes from China to Venice. The ports along the Silk Road will not just act as trade hubs. Gwadar in Pakistan, for example, has potentially been earmarked as a temporary naval base, which may create tensions between China and India in future.

Throughout China's history, trade has been the vehicle for what it dubs cultural exchange and regional collaboration. The reasons for being more explicit about those ambitions now may well be associated with the somewhat isolationist stance the United States is currently taking towards the WTO, its exit from the Trans-Pacific Partnership (TPP) and its concerns regarding future engagements with NAFTA. China's proposed Regional Comprehensive Economic Partnership (RCEP) is not a substitute for the TPP, and the BRI project is not a free trade area – nor is it a customs union. The BRI simply represents an ambition to provide trade infrastructure across the region; it is not meant to be a vehicle for regional integration.

There are 15 regions apart from China in East Asia, the Middle East and Eurasia that are most obviously within the BRI: China's trade is highly focused on Russia, India and Iran, although Turkmenistan, Kazakhstan and Mongolia are key import partners as well (see figure 9).

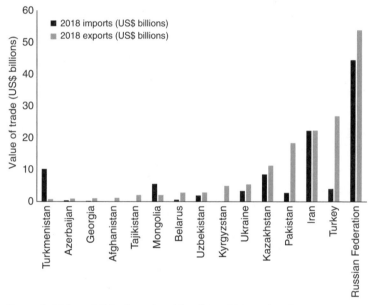

Figure 9. Value of China's trade with selected BRI regional partners, 2016 (US$ billions). *Source:* Coriolis Technologies, 2019.

These are all classified as emerging economies, and yet, including China, the BRI countries' importance as a share of world trade has grown substantially over the past 20 years (see figure 10). Each country has had its own challenges as they have started to integrate into the global trading system. Russia and Iran, for example, have both been subject to UN sanctions, specifically oil embargoes: Russia since 2014, and Iran since 2012. Kazakhstan has similarly been affected by corruption that has undermined its attempts to attract inward investment and grow through trade. Even though trade has receded since 2012 as a result of these challenges, the BRI group of countries represented nearly 34% of world trade in 2016.

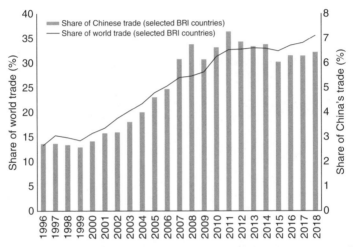

Figure 10. Selected BRI countries' share of world and Chinese trade, 1996–2017 (projected %). *Source:* Coriolis Technologies, 2019.

However, the same group of countries (minus China) only account for a relatively small proportion of China's total trade. Although this proportion has more than doubled since 1996, it is still only just above 6% of China's trade, and highly concentrated in oil and gas.

Is it the case, then, that China's interests are not trade related? The fact that these countries make up such a small proportion of China's trade might suggest so, but a closer look at the data points to just how important these countries are in terms of China's overall supply of energy.

Figure 11 takes the four countries most directly affected by the BRI's Mongolia–Russia route and the proposed Eurasia land bridge: Russia, Iran, Kazakhstan and Mongolia. These countries alone accounted for 17% of China's oil imports in 2016. Again, this share fell after 2012, but the value of imports remained very similar until 2014/2015, when the oil price dropped. This suggests that China's oil demand increased during that period and that it had been met by other sources as well.

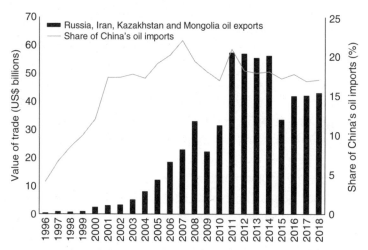

Figure 11. Value of Russia's, Iran's, Kazakhstan's and Mongolia's oil exports to China, 1996–2016 (US$ billions), compared with their share of China's total oil imports (%). *Source:* Coriolis Technologies, 2019.

From a Chinese perspective, more is needed than an update of the infrastructure in this region to reduce the risks to its own energy supply. The routes also provide a cheaper way of transporting goods to Europe while offering countries in the region the potential for infrastructure investment, so their economies can grow and they can overcome some of the political and development issues they have faced. In Xi Jinping's words, China is aiming to demonstrate with the

BRI that it is a 'peace-loving explorer set on transforming the world with treasure-laden galleys not warships, guns or swords'.[162]

In terms of how this plays out at a country level, the case of Kazakhstan is interesting. Kazakhstan has been eager to be at the centre of this policy since it was first announced at a Kazakh university in 2013. The country sees itself as a key corridor between Russia and China, and it has cultural and historical links with both countries. As such, it is something of a cultural integrator between the traditionally nomadic peoples of Kazakhstan, Turkmenistan, Uzbekistan and Mongolia; it is similarly keen to demonstrate that it is independent from Russia, both politically and economically. A country rich in resources, Kazakhstan was the focus of substantial inward investment in oil and gas reserves immediately after the financial crisis, and it is keen to re-establish itself as a major commodity trading nation.

Its regional partners are far less important to it in trade terms than Europe or even China, however (see figure 12). Although China is its second-largest trading partner and its fastest-growing top 10 partner, Kazakhstan's interests are in developing its trade with Europe, particularly Italy.

Annualized growth with European partners since the initiative was launched has been substantial: with Italy, its largest partner, the rate of growth has averaged nearly 22% since 1996, and with the Netherlands it is 21%. This is because of the importance of Kazakhstan's oil and gas supplies, and it reinforces the perspective that this country has much to gain from land-based infrastructure that connects it more easily and cheaply with Europe. Interestingly, its fastest-growing top 10 partner has been Switzerland. This reflects Switzerland's importance as a financial hub through which commodity deals are booked, rather than the amount of direct trade it conducts with Kazakhstan.

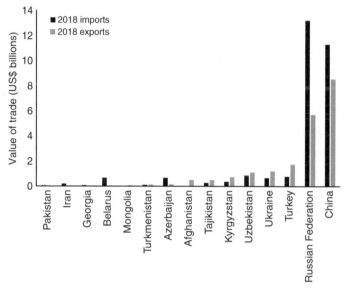

Figure 12. Kazakhstan's top 10 export partners, 2016 (US$ billions). *Source:* Coriolis Technologies, 2019.

The importance of Russia and China in terms of proximity is obvious, and these two nations dwarf the others in terms of their importance to Kazakhstan. Its fastest-growing partners have been, with the notable exceptions of India and Ukraine, in the immediate proximity of its borders. This suggests that some form of economic partnership through BRI policy – if not free trade, then at least an infrastructure partnership – may benefit all the countries. This is not least because they are all oil and gas producers with strong relationships in Europe, China and Russia. The case of Kazakhstan shows how one country, which has stumbled in terms of its trade integration with the rest of the world in recent years, can form closer, potentially multilateral, trade and infrastructure arrangements with its regional partners that may help it to reach bigger markets in Europe.

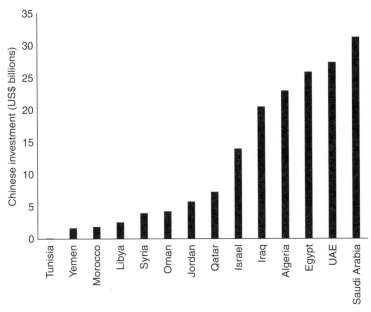

Figure 13. Chinese inward investment, 2005–2018, selected MENA countries. *Source:* Atlantic Council, 2019.[163]

The BRI is increasingly extending into the Middle East and North Africa (MENA) as well, but it is likely that it will prove a double-edged sword for the region. China has increased its investment in the region since 2005, with a particular focus on Saudi Arabia, the United Arab Emirates (UAE), Egypt and Algeria (see figure 13).

The biggest oil exporters are clearly the winners here, but China's strategic investment in the region is likely to be more politically significant. The BRI is the embodiment of China's foreign policy stance: that conflict and disputes are less likely if every economy is growing and individuals have access to the wealth being produced. China sees itself as exporting its own economic model to countries that may benefit from investment. While this has created a heavy debt burden in places such as Pakistan and Sri Lanka, the Chinese attitude is that the long-term prospect of growth outweighs the short-term problem of debt. As the BRI is not scheduled to be completed until 2049, this is a *very* long-term ambition.

Meanwhile, the political challenges the BRI could bring to the MENA region cannot be understated. At present, the proposed route goes north of the Gulf through Kazakhstan before heading into Iran and across to Greece. Investments in Iran or Pakistan could heighten some of the tensions between Saudi Arabia and Iran. The sea route passes by the Horn of Africa, up the Red Sea and through the Suez Canal. These are highly sensitive areas, and the fact that China has proposed US$15 million in economic aid to the Palestinians and US$90 million for reconstruction and economic development in Syria, Yemen, Jordan and Lebanon could create unease. This will not just be felt within the region; it has the potential to spill into the global dispute between the United States and China, as the investments could be interpreted as being politically motivated.

The biggest considerations for Saudi Arabia and the UAE will centre around their existing debt burden and their desire for increased inward investment. Saudi Arabia is in the weaker position, having acquired greater long-term debt than the UAE, but both countries have invested heavily in developing trade with China over the last five years and will be reluctant to hamper that progress.

It is estimated that around US$210 billion of the originally planned US$1 trillion of BRI investment has already been spent, predominantly across Asia.[164] However, the hubris initially surrounding the BRI has abated since it became explicit Chinese policy in 2013. Countries such as Malaysia and Pakistan have paused to review their participation, as their own fiscal challenges have the potential to become more acute with greater involvement. The Chinese Marshall Plan is focused on mutual economic development, and yet, in some countries, Chinese firms are seen to be benefiting over and above local ones.

Within the MENA region, unemployment is under-reported and is possibly higher than public records state. Because this region also suffers from insurgencies and popular uprisings, inward investment from China linked to Chinese businesses may not provide the answers that policymakers are currently seeking. This is particularly the case for some of the most heavily invested countries, such as Algeria, Saudi Arabia and Egypt, where unemployment is currently at 11.6%, 12.9% and 10.9%, respectively.

Is there a game to win?

As we have seen, the United States and China have entirely different approaches to foreign policy. For the United States, the goal is to win and win quickly. This is partly a function of the electoral cycle, of course. For China, as Henry Kissinger explains it, foreign policy is 'conceptual'. In other words, it can take a long time to formulate and implement: winning is not the explicit objective, although it is still deeply nationalist. Here, the goals are to grow the dominance of the CPC through the welfare of Chinese citizens, defend Chinese sovereignty and interests, and drive economic development. To this extent, Xi's socialism with Chinese characteristics is little different to China's dominant objective during the 1980–2012 period: communism with a capitalist view.

China's strategy, then, as highlighted in the BRI, is to protect its own economic growth against risks, including the risk of defaults across the BRI region by providing loans to countries such as Pakistan and Sri Lanka in aid of the ports and infrastructures that are being developed. This is simply securitized foreign policy, which the world, and particularly the United States, has not been used to.

The problem China faces because of Xi's influence and intolerance of dissent (or 'corruption'), either domestically or in the country's semi-autonomous regions, is that what people are seeing from the outside is a scheme focused on power and control, not a plan to achieve multilateral growth on the basis of shared goals. China still needs the rest of the world, which currently mistrusts it, and there are several elements that would ultimately limit the extent to which it could ever engage in a military conflict.

First, China is effectively 'buying' its power.[165] Much of the BRI's future success will depend on it. This is not because China is not committed to the project, or because China does not have the ambition to grow its influence through trade by connecting Europe to Asia through its twenty-first-century Silk Road. The initiative could help China, too: in 2013 it was oversupplying infrastructure products, which, as its strategy changed towards demand-led growth, created a surplus that could be manufactured elsewhere. Since then, it has run down its foreign currency reserves, and while it wants to share the benefits of its own export-led model, the economic regions surrounding it do not possess the same financial clout that China had when it was a developing country in the heady days of globalization.

China itself is also lacking that financial clout now. The country is wary of capital flight as its economy grows more slowly. The Asia Infrastructure Investment Bank (AIIB) and the New Development Bank (formerly the BRICS Development Bank) have US$200 billion between them, but this is only a fraction of the amount that will be required to fund the project on the scale currently imagined. A further US$40 billion from the Silk Road Fund is also a mere drop in the ocean.

Second, China has explicitly stated that it cannot 'go it alone': the challenges of the world are too big for the country to be able to achieve its ambitions solo. So much of the short- and medium-term success of the BRI will depend on the appetite among global banks and investors for funding infrastructure developments in some of the world's most difficult (from a compliance perspective) countries: nations that score highly on corruption and political instability indices, and for which the trade values are small. In the current global trade climate, these are significant hurdles.

China will need to open its financial markets to overseas investors and businesses if the BRI is to work. In the end, this will mean it is supporting peace and stability in the fragile countries where it is building, including by giving more work to local employees and by allowing local contractors into its projects. China will also have to not only open its own banks to supporting overseas businesses, as its own credit agency has done, but also allow overseas credit agencies to work alongside Chinese investors.

Third, it is not in China's interests to help trigger the demise of global institutions such as the IMF and the WTO, both of which helped it to build its economic power in the first place. This means that it will have to fall in line with WTO obligations and rules if it is to prevent the United States from developing dispute settlement rules on its own terms.

China is aware of its weaknesses as well as its strengths, and that, perhaps, explains why its strategy is currently being misread. At an International Chamber of Commerce (ICC) Banking Commission event in Beijing in April 2019, concerns about how this trade war was affecting businesses across the country were abundant. Many articulated that SMEs who were exporting to the United States had gone out of business, and – off the record – some expressed unease about the size of Chinese debt. The trade war is affecting the role of global businesses in the country because China is both a market and a resource (financially); if it weakens in either regard, this will encourage companies to move to other countries in the region where the requirements for local content and access to finance are not so stringent. While trade finance priced in renminbi was beginning to increase when the ICC Banking Commission event was held, this was not viewed as something that would have an immediate impact on currency markets.

Sun Tzu's advice was to 'appear weak when you are strong and strong when you are weak'. This may reflect the reality of China's current position in relation to the BRI, since it is facing manifest problems in the near term that could impair both foreign and domestic policymakers. As for the long term, it is worth remembering how Sun Tzu's philosophy was translated into the overarching principle of Chinese foreign policy by Deng Xiaoping: 'hide your brightness, bide your time'.[166]

Overall, it is the trust issue that is China's greatest hurdle right now. To counter this, its partners need to be assured of its reliability.[167] We do not know what game China is playing; by using powerful language and engaging in tit-for-tat brinkmanship with the United States, it is possible that, as elsewhere, we are watching the basketball game and not the gorilla. China's approach in the past has been pragmatic. Any changes in foreign policy have been instigated by external events, and China's more-vocal stance has been noticeable since the financial crisis, not just Xi's accession to power. Sun Tzu and Deng would perhaps feel uncomfortable with this type of explicit power play – even if it is only a distraction – not least because it increases the chance of miscalculation on all sides.

Table 5. China and the United States: multilayer games.

		US	
		US imposes tariffs	US does not escalate
CHINA	China imposes tariffs	Both sides lose	US loses, China wins
	China does not escalate	US wins, China loses	Both sides win
Known unknowns			

Table 5 shows Chinese strategy from a game theory perspective. Superficially, China is matching the United States' tariffs tit-for-tat. This table is broadly like the one seen in chapter 3, as China has taken steps to play the United States at its own game by imposing reciprocal tariffs. However, China's matrix has one key difference: the outer box that surrounds the matrix with the title 'Known unknowns'. China is clearly playing the long game, and it is probable the country will engage with the United States in an attritional trade war for as long as they need to. Meanwhile, it has a number of options at its disposal that transcend the zero-sum approach to strategic trade being employed by the US administration. We mentioned previously the similarities between each state's strategies and national board games. Here, the analogy is helpful once again. Trump is playing chess: as such, all his pieces are on the board in plain view. His opponent (Xi) is therefore able to make a reasonable assessment as to which pieces will be moved next. Xi, however, is playing *Weiqi*: he is using a longer-term strategy that is unconcerned with immediate attack and decisive victory. Crucially, his game pieces are not on the board but in his hand. Thus, while cognizant of the fact that he will make a move, his opponent is uncertain as to what exactly that move will be.

Chapter 6

Red flags? Russia's construction of oblique power

Introduction: Russia's hybrid approach

The use of non-conventional means alongside overt military force to gain a strategic advantage through subversion has been dubbed 'hybrid warfare'. It has also been referred to as non-linear, full-spectrum, all-means and ambiguous warfare, to mention but a few of its epithets. The term has been controversial, but it is apt: Russia's current strategic approach, for example, revolves around the concept of mobilizing all of the state's available power structures to pursue political ends. Crucially, the principal objective seems to be to 'achieve politically decisive outcomes with, if possible, no or only a limited and overt use of military force'.[168]

Building power and influence without the need to engage militarily is a crucial aspect of Russia's approach, since by avoiding direct military confrontation they can continue to subvert Western influence without, for example, triggering Article 5 of the NATO treaty. Russia has had several successes with its subversive, irregular approach, and because this country is no less important than the United States or China in the current paradigmatic power struggle, it is vital that we understand how it exploits different strategic dimensions. This is where our concept of strategic trade comes in; much of the West's analysis of Russia's hybrid approach has focused on its tactical and operational levels as well as its application to military strategy. However, according to Russia's interpretation of hybrid war (*gibridnaya voina*), its aims are far broader and relate to 'all spheres of public life: politics, economy, social development, culture'.[169] With that definition in mind, this chapter will focus on Putin's grand strategic vision for Russia and how his use of trade ties in with achieving this.

That a hybrid approach is being employed has become clear through Russia's interactions with Ukraine. On 21 November 2013 former Ukrainian president Viktor Yanukovych announced that he would not be signing an accession agreement, initialled the previous year by members of the EU, that would formalize Ukraine's membership of the EU.[170] That same evening, thousands of pro-EU demonstrators gathered in Kiev's *Maidan Nezalezhnosti* – Independence Square – to protest Yanukovych's lurch away from the West in favour of closer ties with Russia. Protests continued for months and, by February 2014, the so-called Euromaidan movement had escalated into a revolution: government buildings were seized by demonstrators in several cities, and over 20,000 protesters marched on Parliament. On 22 February 2014 Ukrainian Members of Parliament voted to impeach Yanukovych, who fled the country the following day. Just three days later (26 February), and with the world distracted by the events unfolding in Kiev, reports began coming in that the now infamous 'little green men' – mysterious masked

soldiers carrying high-tech weaponry but no military insig-
nia – had been spotted on the Crimean Peninsula.[171] Several
weeks later, Russian and Crimean representatives signed
the Treaty on Accession of the Republic of Crimea to Russia
as Western leaders looked on in disbelief. This marked the
first annexation of a sovereign territory in Europe since the
end of World War II.

The deployment of military forces was merely the final
stage in a complex strategy involving information warfare,
voter manipulation, cyberattacks, political subversion and
economic coercion. Indeed, just nine months before the first
protests broke out in Kiev, Valery Gerasimov – Chief of the
General Staff of the Armed Forces of Russia – had written an
influential article titled 'The value of science in foresight'. In
it, he argues that a successful strategy should blend non-military and military measures at a ratio of roughly 4:1, with
overt military force comprising only a small fraction of the
strategy.[172]

In the modern era, Gerasimov explains, the challenge
is setting appropriate limits on the use of military force. In
keeping with this strategy, the annexation of Crimea was
completed with minimal bloodshed: just two Ukrainian soldiers lost their lives. Russia employed similar methods in its
war with Georgia in 2008. More recently, it has pursued an
analogous approach in the Donbass region of eastern Ukraine,
often with limited direct military involvement from Moscow.
As Charles K. Bartles writes, 'the important point is that while
the West considers these non-military measures as ways of
avoiding war, Russia considers these measures as war'.[173] Russia's subversive approach has proven extremely effective in
probing the limits of the West's resolve.

Russia's strategic objectives:
Putin the 'reactionary restorer'?

Putin's principal strategic objective is the 'restoration, association, [and] unification' of Russia. He famously referred to
the collapse of the Soviet Union as the greatest geopolitical
catastrophe of the century,[174] as it effectively left millions of
former Soviet citizens outside of Russia's 'sphere of influence'. Putin's desire for the restoration of Russian greatness
is well documented. When coupled with his aim of reviving
some form of Russian empire, Putin's subversive attempts to
prevent the integration of former Soviet states into the West
(either the EU or NATO) begin to make more sense. However,
the use of overt and excessive military means in pursuit of
this end will only provoke a corresponding response from
NATO. Thus, the challenge for Russia is to undermine Western
influence without arousing suspicion or executing any action
that may trigger Article 5.

Thus, trade provides a useful strategic option: exporting goods to countries with separatist movements (such
as Ukraine, Georgia or Moldova) can help destabilize them
while Russia maintains 'implausible deniability'. Equally, the
supply of dual-use goods to areas of the world that could be
strategically important, either now or in the future, helps
to build 'strategic potential'. The civilian applications of
dual-use goods allow their export to slip under the radar
of suspicion, which means Russia can build its influence in
key strategic locations (e.g. by exporting naval goods to
partners around the Black Sea) with a view to augmenting
its capabilities or asserting itself as the dominant military
power in these regions. In addition, supplying the materials
for ballistic missile programmes to adversaries of the United

States (e.g. Iran or Cuba) serves as an effective 'destabilizer' by forcing the United States to take action, thereby putting them on the back foot. If an empire is the ultimate objective, asks Russian journalist Alexei Venediktov, 'where will we stop? In Syria? In Africa? In Canada!? What are the limits to the "Russian" world?'[175]

What follows are three short case studies that demonstrate Russia's attempts to exploit the globalized economic system and pursue a strategy that furthers its own interests while undermining those of the West. The first case study, which looks at Russia's trade relationship with Syria, demonstrates how Russia facilitated the transition of the Syrian economy to a war footing[176] and generated a tragic humanitarian situation that has distracted the Western security community from its growing naval influence in Tartus. The second case study looks at Russia's role in Ukraine prior to and during the 2014 revolution. It concludes that Russia may have been providing materials for weapon production to the Luhansk weapons factory in eastern Ukraine for months before the crisis broke out.

The third case study examines Russia's supply of goods to Iran for missile development. This reflects a strategy of bolstering the latter's efforts to create a more efficient programme and, coupled with Russia's involvement in Syria, undermines Western (and specifically US) efforts to achieve regional stability.

Russia is clearly using the globalized trading system to its advantage by fuelling separatist movements, propping up regimes, funding missile programmes and building strategic potential in the Black Sea. This negates the argument that trade is limited to the realms of either hard or soft power and demonstrates that it can be used coercively or integratively, e.g. via 'selective trade embargoes'. In the sense that it is employing unconventional, indirect means to influence outcomes, Russia's current approach bears many of the hallmarks of hybrid warfare along with a more general strategy of building power through indirect engagements.

Case study 1: Russia and the Syrian war

Transition of the economy to a war footing

There is a misconception in the literature that economic methods of gaining power simply involve coercion through sanctions or embargoes. Gerasimov's theory shows an additional, often overlooked, aspect of these methods: facilitating the 'transition of a state's economy to a war footing'.[177] The instability that ensues from sending a country's economy in such a direction allows the exporting state (in this case, Russia) to achieve its desired political ends while the country in question and its wider international community are distracted by the deteriorating security situation.

Putin's open support for the Assad regime in Syria is well documented, and Russia's military intervention in September 2015 has seen Assad regain control over the core of the country (at time of writing). However, Russia's support is clearly not due to any political alliance it has with Syria. The latter's western coastline looks out onto the Mediterranean Sea. Thus, the port city of Tartus, the second-largest port in Syria, is a key strategic location. In January 2017 Russia signed a 49-year deal that granted it full control of the naval base in Tartus, which is capable of hosting up to 11 warships. Through a series of charts, this section will show how Russia has fuelled

Syria's war through the provision of arms, ammunition and explosives as well as via Sector 99.[i]

At the end of 2010 and throughout 2011 widespread pro-democracy protests broke out across the Middle East and North Africa. The causes of the so-called Arab Spring were numerous, but the main grievances of the protesters were political repression, endemic corruption, human rights violations, high rates of poverty and poor employment prospects. In Syria, the protests escalated to a devastating civil war. On 15 March 2011 thousands took to the streets of Damascus to oppose President Bashar al-Assad. Their protests intensified after Assad's forces opened fire on them: protesters began arming themselves in response and soon split into several rebel groups who violently opposed the Assad regime. As the war progressed, the conflict developed a sectarian element as Sunni Muslims clashed with Alawites and the Islamic State grew in influence. According to Amnesty International, since 2011 roughly 250,000 Syrians have lost their lives and more than 11 million have been displaced.[178]

Sanctions against Bashar al-Assad also took their toll as members of the international community ceased trading with a regime they could not support. The economy has all

i While there is no formal definition on the UN website of the goods that belong to Sector 99, analysis often shows statistically significant increases in state imports of goods from this sector immediately prior to the onset of political upheaval and crisis. Sector 99's vital statistics are as follows. First, its total value in 2016 was around US$113 billion, or nearly 6% of world trade. Second, the correlation coefficient between dual-use goods trade and Sector 99 is 0.91. Third, the correlation coefficient between arms trade and commodities not elsewhere specified is 0.77. Fourth, it is Russia's largest export sector, and, between February and March 2014 in Ukraine (when Crimea was annexed), trade in this sector increased from US$587,000 to US$774.4 million before falling by May to US$244,000.

but collapsed as fighting has intensified (see figure 14). In 2010 Syria's imports were valued at nearly US$22 billion, and its exports were worth US$12.5 billion. By 2012 this had dropped to US$7.6 billion for imports and US$2.1 billion for exports, declines of 65% and 83%, respectively.[ii]

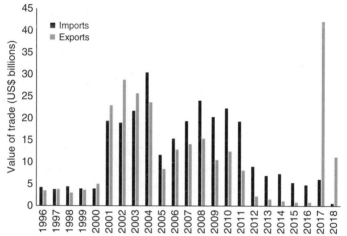

Figure 14. Value of Syria's import and export trade with the world, US$ millions. *Source:* Coriolis Technologies.

This chart also shows that, even post-2012, Syria was still importing goods at a rate comparable to that of 1996–2000. What has changed, however, is the nature of the goods that are entering the country.

According to Gerasimov's model, nudging a state towards a war footing is critical in influencing the outcome of

---

ii The spike in 2017 is remarkable and can be accounted for by fruit and vegetable exports to Lebanon. The spike in Lebanese imports in 2017 is also a function of imports from China, Austria, Italy and France. This may be a statistical aberration, but it is important to bear in mind that in Syria's case this corresponds to the end of the battles against ISIS insurgents and an embryonic progression towards economic recovery.

any conflict in that state.[179] In 2014 Jihad Yazigi wrote that Syria had transitioned to a war economy and that the type of goods being supplied to the country were simply prolonging the conflict, while regime-controlled areas enjoyed 'the provision of many basic state services'.[180] Figure 15, which compares Russian and US trade with Syria, demonstrates how Russia has supplied a significant proportion of these imports. In 2011 the proportion of Syria's trade accounted for by the United States fell from 3% to 2.5%. In 2012, as America pursued a strategy of trying to hamstring the Assad campaign through economic sanctions, it was just 0.4%. Conversely, Russian trade with Syria increased from 7% of the total value in 2010 to 10.7% when war broke out. It rose again in 2012 to 11.5% as Russia continued to supply the regime forces with arms.

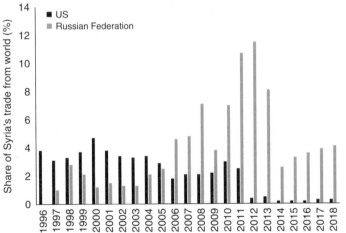

Figure 15.   Percentage of total trade: the United States and Russia compared, 1996–2018. *Sources:* Coriolis Technologies, own analysis.

Russia's trade profile with Syria changed between 2009 (before the conflict began) and 2013 (see table 6). Sector 99 (defined as 'commodities not elsewhere specified'), explosives, and arms and ammunition accounted for just 0.3% of Russia's exports to Syria in 2000, when Putin began his first term as President of Russia. By 2010, the year before the conflict, this had increased to 44.5% of the total value. This rose to 52.7% in 2011 and reached a high of 76.2% in 2012.

Table 6. Russia's arms and explosives exports to Syria as a percentage of Syria's total trade (2009–2013). *Source:* Coriolis Technologies.

Year	Russia's arms, explosives; Sector 99 exports to Syria (as % of Syria's total trade)
2009	7.3
2010	44.5
2011	52.7
2012	76.2
2013	72.4

The devastation in Syria is arguably of little concern to Russia, since the Assad regime now controls the entire west coast of the country, allowing Russia to begin augmenting the capabilities of Tartus as a base while the conflict continues, and to limit the West's strategic options by creating a naval 'no-go zone' off the coast of Syria. Further, the tragic humanitarian situation will distract the international community from the comparatively less important construction of a few naval vessels in a port that Russia has maintained since 1971.

Trade is acting as a proxy, hiding something deeper, and the West (particularly NATO) should be paying close attention to Russia's bolstering of its naval capabilities and its improvements to infrastructure on Tartus. Syria's war has provided Russia with a testing ground for submarine-launched variants of the Kalibr missile. There are over a dozen variants of the missile, many of them ground or ship launched, but 8 December 2015 saw the first operational use of the 3M-14 Kalibr missile against targets in Syria. According to Jane's Information Group, the development is a 'game changer' since this variant of the missile has a payload of around 500 kg, with an estimated range of between 1,500 and 2,000 km and accuracy to within 'a few meters'.[181] According to Putin, the missile 'can be equipped either with conventional or special nuclear warheads'.[182] This lends an even greater sense of urgency to evidence from Coriolis Technologies trade data that there have been significant increases in Russia's exports of marine equipment to former Soviet states around the Black Sea: specifically, Bulgaria, Georgia, Albania, Moldova and, crucially, Ukraine.

Case study 2: Russia and Ukraine

The context to the crisis – 'Little Russians' and the Black Sea

Russia's historical relationship with Ukraine is long and complex. It is perhaps best summarized by a comment made by Putin to former US president George W. Bush at a NATO summit in Bucharest: 'You have to understand, George, that the Ukraine is not even a country. Part of its territory is in eastern Europe and the greater part was given to us.'[183] This imperial mindset, rejected by Ukrainian nationalists, stems from the interwoven history of Ukraine and Russia for the best part of a thousand years. From the late 1700s, Russia began referring to the left and right banks of Ukraine as 'Malaya Rossiya' (Малая Россия): Little Russia.

Russia has held control over these areas since then, imposing bans on the use of the Ukrainian language and the publication of

Ukrainian nationalist texts. The collapse of the Russian Empire in 1917 and the bloody civil war that followed temporarily ended its rule of Ukraine, but in 1922 the creation of the Union of Soviet Socialist Republics (USSR) saw much of Ukraine integrated once more. While referring to Ukraine as 'Little Russia' and to Ukrainians as 'Little Russians' has fallen out of usage in Ukraine itself, within Russia these terms are still frequently heard. This is indicative of the attitude held by many Russians: Ukraine is, and always will be, part of Russia. Any attempts by Ukraine to work more closely with the EU or NATO have been met with fierce opposition and thinly veiled warnings.

The war in Georgia showed Russia's willingness to protect its interests. In a warning that would precede the academic attention currently being afforded to hybrid warfare, General Baluyevsky stated that the measures taken to do so would be not only military but also 'steps of a different nature',[184] including coercive economics, or – as we are arguing here – strategic trade. Russia's approach has been to use embargoes because Ukraine is heavily reliant on Russia's supply of oil and gas.

Russian exports have accounted for most of Ukraine's oil and gas imports since 1997. However, in 2006 an oil and gas pricing dispute led to Russia shutting off its supply to Ukraine for close to a year. As a result, Ukrainian imports from Russia in this sector totalled just US$407 million in that period. A political crisis erupted following Europe's attempts to mediate and resolve the dispute, leading to the collapse of Ukraine's more EU-oriented 'Orange' government. The gas dispute clearly demonstrated the extent of the political leverage that Moscow could exert over Kiev. A second gas dispute in 2009 had similar motives: this was aimed at disrupting President Viktor Yushchenko's objective of forming closer ties with the EU and NATO by showing Ukraine to be an unreliable, politically and economically unstable ally. However, the election of a more pro-Russian candidate, Viktor Yanukovych, as president in 2010 ensured Ukraine was more likely to toe the line. These warmer relations with Russia are reflected in the trade data. However, we see a drop in oil and gas exports after the Ukrainian crisis in 2014, with Russia's exports declining from US$10.8 billion in 2013 to US$4.1 billion in 2014, hitting a low of US$202 million in 2017 (see figure 16).

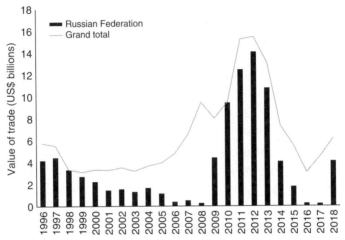

Figure 16. Ukraine gas imports from world and Russia compared, 1997–2018. *Source:* Coriolis Technologies.

Building strategic potential

Since at least 2010, Russia has deployed trade in a less coercive manner against Ukraine, leaning instead towards a strategy of building strategic potential through the export of dual-use goods. This trend began with the election of Russia's 'man in Kiev' Viktor Yanukovych. Yanukovych was elected President of

Ukraine on 7 February 2010, beating his rival and former co-leader of the Orange Revolution, Yulia Tymoshenko, by 48.95% to 45.47%. Yanukovych was Moscow's preferred candidate, and, as vote maps of the election show, he won the presidency on the strength of his support from the more pro-Russian east of Ukraine. Although Yanukovych declared that 'Ukraine's integration with the EU remains our strategic aim', the reality was that Putin now had an ally who shared his vision for a closer relationship.

This relationship is reflected in Ukraine's trade profile. The percentage share of Russia's total trade (i.e. the total value in US dollars of its exports and imports) increased from 13.4% in 2009 to 18.2% in 2010. In value terms, this constitutes an increase of US$10.1 billion. Meanwhile, the proportion of total trade accounted for by the EU over the same period declined from 20.1% in 2009 to 19.3% in 2010.[185] Through Yanukovych, Putin successfully negotiated an extension for Russia's Black Sea Fleet at Sevastopol until 2042 and guaranteed that Ukraine would not join NATO. In exchange, Russia offered Ukraine a 30% subsidy on Ukrainian gas prices. Figure 17 shows how between January and March 2010 marine goods accounted for 83.4% of Russia's total dual-use goods exports to Ukraine, clear evidence that Russia was attempting to augment the capabilities of its naval base at Sevastopol.

Naval power will be essential in asserting Russian dominance. Figure 17 examines one particular dual-use goods sector: 'marine'. This category has 162 subsectors, including floating docks, special purpose vessels, marine propulsion engines, propellers, transmission shafts, gears and 'other' vessels (including military vessels and submarines). In March 2014 it accounted for 51.8% of Russia's exports to Ukraine. Indeed, on a monthly basis (from January 2010 to September 2018) the marine sector has accounted for, on average, 14.9% of Russia's dual-use goods exports to Ukraine. However, the most interesting increase was in February 2010, when it accounted for 83.4%.

Just a few months before this increase, the former Ukrainian government had released a statement that the lease of Russian naval bases on the Crimea would not be extended beyond 2017; so, in response, the Black Sea Fleet initiated an expansion of its base in Novorossiysk and, through the targeted export of marine goods, attempted to build strategic potential for the future. We see similarly large increases in dual-use goods in March and April 2014, the months of the annexation of the Crimea. Again, this was in response to the escalating conflict in Ukraine and the uncertainty surrounding future opportunities to trade with this country.

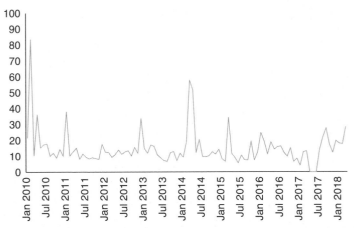

Figure 17. Russia's 'marine' exports to Ukraine as percentage of total dual-use goods, January 2010–January 2018. *Source:* Coriolis Technologies.

Despite Ukraine's warmer relations with Russia under Yanukovych's presidency, an Association Agreement (AA) with the EU was still in the works. On 30 March 2012 the EU formally entered into an AA with Ukraine in order to establish closer political and economic ties. Putin voiced his concerns over the arrangement, stating that he felt it was a 'major threat' to Russian economic security. He privately requested that Yanukovych delay signing.[186] In March 2013 Yanukovych took steps to withdraw from the agreement, and by November he had announced that plans were suspended indefinitely. Officially, Yanukovych stated that Ukraine could not afford to abandon Russia, as the economic impact would be too great. The damage was already done, however, and thousands of pro-EU supporters rallied on the streets of Kiev. Three months later, Yanukovych was forced to flee the country.

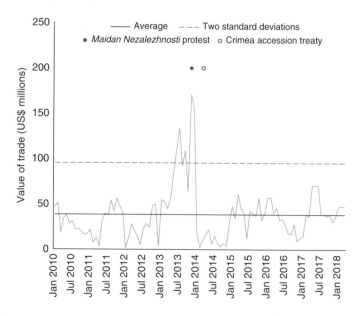

Figure 18. Russia's dual-use goods exports to Ukraine, January 2010–January 2018. *Source:* Coriolis Technologies. *Note:* The data shows clear evidence of Russia's strategic intent in Ukraine prior to the outbreak of the crisis. Monitoring unusual activity in dual-use goods would have provided an indication of a crisis brewing between June and July 2013.

In the months leading up to the crisis, while Yanukovych was stalling on signing the AA, Russia was surreptitiously exporting substantial volumes of dual-use goods to Ukraine (see figure 18). These exports were predominantly marine equipment, special items and nuclear materials.

This bolsters the idea that Russia was building its strategic potential by stockpiling materials related to submarine-launched missile development using the Crimea and its naval base at Sevastopol. Incredibly, the Coriolis Technologies model identified statistically significant increases in exports (i.e. above two standard deviations) a full *five months* before the first Euromaidan protest. Russia was clearly preparing for a potentially violent public response to Ukraine abandoning ties with the EU as well as uncertainty over how successfully and with what restrictions it would be able to trade with Ukraine in the future. Interestingly, the increases began just two months after Valery Gerasimov published his article on a modern approach to warfare, perhaps an indication that Russia was beginning to explore alternative strategic options using trade.

The War in Donbass: supplying the separatists

The War in Donbass began in April 2014 when a group of pro-Russian separatists stormed the offices of the Security Service of Ukraine (SBU) in Luhansk and Donetsk as well as the Ministry of Internal Affairs in Donetsk. The situation escalated when separatists began expanding the territory under their control, seizing government buildings in cities across eastern Ukraine such as Mariupol, Sloviansk, Druzhkivka, Kramatorsk and Zhdanivka. On 4 May they raised a flag above the police headquarters in the city and declared the Donetsk People's Republic. The Ukrainian government carried out a counteroffensive and removed separatist forces from many of the strategic locations they had occupied across the Donetsk Oblast. Nevertheless, fighting worsened throughout the year and several ceasefires failed to take hold. As of 13 June 2019, the UN estimates between 12,800 and 13,000 people have lost their lives in the fighting, with around 1.5 million people displaced.[187]

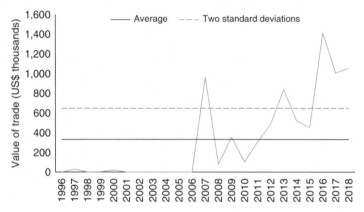

Figure 19. Russia's use of steel U-sections <80mm to Ukraine, 1996–2018. *Source:* Coriolis Technologies.

Russia's role in the crisis is now a matter of public record. Putin has retracted previous statements regarding his 'little green men' and has now admitted they are members of Russia's special forces. A report conducted by Conflict Armament Research concluded that: 'It is **very likely** that pro-Russian separatist groups have received some level of support (including small arms, light weapons, guided light weapons, heavier weapons systems, and armoured vehicles) from one or more external parties.'[188]

Unsurprisingly, data on the arms trade between Russia and Ukraine before the crisis is fairly unhelpful. According to the information available, Russia all but ceased trading in arms with Ukraine from 2013. The Coriolis Technologies database shows that Russian exports in this sector exhibit a year-on-year decrease of 82.9% between 2014 and 2013, falling to zero thereafter. This is hardly news given that Russia has long pursued a strategy of maintaining deniability (however implausible). Even clearly identifiable Russian factory markings on any weapons supplied to Ukraine have been challenging to find. Instead, we have uncovered evidence that Russia pursued a strategy of providing the means for Ukrainian separatists to assemble and repair their own rifles (many of which are Cold War models and variants of the Kalashnikov) prior to the outbreak of the crisis.

Photographs of separatists operating in the Donbass have revealed that the older AK-74 model of assault rifle is frequently being used in the conflict.[189] The AK-74 replaced the AKM model in 1973, but, according to a technical description, 'the receiver remains nearly identical to that of the AKM; it is a U-shaped 1 mm (0.04 in) thick sheet steel pressing supported extensively by pins and rivets'.[190] Of all the six-digit Harmonized System code sectors in iron and steel, there is just one that fits the description of a U-shaped steel sheet: 'U, I or H sections, not further worked than hot-rolled, hot-drawn or extruded, of a height of less than 80 mm'. Interestingly, if we analyse Russian exports in this sector, we can see that there was an increase of 58.3% in 2013 and a further increase of 71.8% in 2014. This is despite trade with Ukraine collapsing after 2013 in almost every other sector.

Figure 19 demonstrates three significant spikes (i.e. above two standard deviations), with each increase occurring prior to the political crises in 2008/09, 2013/14 and the escalation of conflict in the Donbass region in 2016/17.

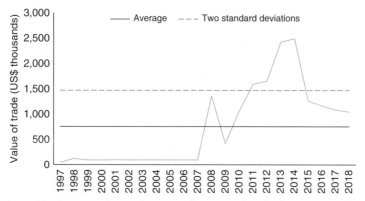

Figure 20. Copper plates, sheets and strips of a thickness exceeding 0.15 mm; of 'copper-zinc base alloys (brass) :– other' to Ukraine, 1996–2018. *Source:* Coriolis Technologies.

Figure 20 tells a similar story. In 2013 and 2014 Russia exported to Ukraine in 23 copper-related sectors, from 'copper alloys :– copper-zinc base alloys (brass)', to 'table, kitchen or other household articles and parts thereof; pot scourers and scouring or polishing pads, gloves and the like :– other'. However, of these 23 sectors, only two saw consecutive percentage increases in 2013 and 2014. The first was 'copper-tin base alloys (bronze) :– other', which experienced increases of 9.4% in 2013 and 3.7% in 2014. However, the data shows that the values involved were insignificant (just US$11,200 in 2013 and US$11,600 in 2014). The second was 'copper-zinc base alloys (brass) :– other', specifically copper plates, sheets and strips of a thickness exceeding 0.15 mm. This sector saw year-on-year increases of 46.4% in 2013 and 2.7% in 2014, representing values of US$2.4 million and US$2.5 million, respectively.

The significance of the increases in this sector is that this grade of copper is used in the production of Kalashnikov assault rifle casings, and, as a result, it is usually referred to as 'cartridge brass'.[191] Further, analysis of round casings found in the Donbass by war correspondents attached to *The New York Times* revealed that, of the more modern casings discovered,[iii] each bore the stamp ЛПЗ (LPZ): the marking of the weapons factory in Luhansk.[192] Although Ukroboronprom accounted for 100% of government contracts at the end of 2014, separatists managed to capture Ukraine's only small arms manufacturing plant – located in Luhansk – in March 2014. Luhansk is the eastern-most Ukrainian state and has strong historical connections with both the USSR and Russia. The data clearly shows substantial increases (significantly above two standard deviations) in trade in sectors used in arms and ammunition manufacturing prior to, and during, the outbreak of the political crisis.

By exporting in these two sectors, neither of which are currently classified as dual-use goods, instead of directly exporting arms and ammunition, Russia can influence outcomes in the War in Donbass while maintaining some level of deniability. Further, trade in these sectors tends to slip under the radar of the international community, who have, until recently, failed to acknowledge the significance of trade in strategy and the construction of power. However, Russia's trade in dual-use goods is a central feature of its hybrid approach, and it warrants much closer international attention, as our next case study will show.

Case study 3: Russia and the Iranian ballistic missile programme

Minimize US power, maximize Russian power

The final way in which Russia uses strategic trade is by providing goods to support other states' missile and nuclear

---

iii Rounds produced post the collapse of the Soviet Union.

programmes. The broader strategic aim of this is to undermine US hegemony by giving America yet another urgent problem to deal with. It is particularly important given current tensions in the Middle East.

On 15 July 2015 the P5+1 of the UN Security Council (the United States, Russia, China, the United Kingdom and France, plus Germany) reached an agreement with Iran that it would 'under no circumstances ever seek, develop or acquire any nuclear weapons' in exchange for sanctions relief.[193] The agreement, known as the Joint Comprehensive Plan of Action (JCPOA) or, more commonly, the 'Iran nuclear deal', is to remain in place until 2030. However, on 10 October 2015 Iran carried out a successful test of its Emad missile: this is a medium-range ballistic missile with an estimated range of 2,000 km, a payload of 750 kg and the potential to be fitted with a nuclear warhead. Although the test came as a surprise to many, it did not technically violate the terms of the JCPOA given that no nuclear materials were involved.

Many Western critics have argued, however, that while this test does not technically contravene the terms of the JCPOA, it does violate those of UN Security Council Resolution 2231, which was adopted on 20 July 2015 – just five days later. Resolution 2231 states: 'Iran is called upon not to undertake any activity related to ballistic missiles designed to be capable of delivering nuclear weapons, including launches using such ballistic missile technology'. Iran's response, however, was that it is under no obligation to conform to the Resolution, given that 'calling upon' someone to do something is not a legal requirement but a suggestion; as such, it should be free to carry out missile tests. Using this interpretation, in the two years between August 2015 and August 2017, Iran carried out at least 23 ballistic missile launches (including operations, tests and drills). According to the Foundation for Defense of Democracies (FDD), around 16 of the missiles launched were, in theory, nuclear capable.[194]

There are three key points to understand regarding the development of Iran's ballistic and nuclear missile programme: first, Iran possesses the 'most diverse ballistic-missile arsenal in the Middle East'. Second, ballistic missiles are 'central to Iran's deterrence posture and will remain so for the foreseeable future'.[195] Third, Iran is not pursuing a ballistic missile programme unilaterally; over the last few years, it has had substantial help from Russia.

The Soviet Union was the first state to recognize Iran as an Islamic republic, but relations between the two countries have not always been smooth. In 1980 war broke out between Iran and Iraq after Ruhollah Khomeini called for an Islamic revolution in Iraq to overthrow Saddam Hussein's secular Ba'ath Party. Hussein responded by launching an invasion of Iran on 22 September 1980, following up airstrikes with a large-scale ground invasion. From the Soviets' perspective, Khomeini's Islamic regime was incompatible with the irreligious communist ideals of the USSR. As a result, they supplied the secular Hussein with arms.

Since the 1990s relations have been far more cordial: Russia has even made significant contributions to the development of Iran's nuclear programme by providing materials and its own expertise. It was thanks to Russian support that Iran managed to complete its first nuclear reactor – Bushehr I – in 2011. In fact, Iran and Russia are finding themselves increasingly politically aligned. To be clear, this is not a deep friendship but a marriage of convenience: a strategic partnership with the purpose of limiting US global hegemony, which, according to Russia's 2015 NSS, is 'exerting a negative influence on the realization of Russian national interests'.[196]

From Russia's perspective, a nuclear-capable state in the Middle East is a serious threat to US power in the region, and although Russia certainly does not want to provoke nuclear war (Putin even encouraged Tehran to remain in the JCPOA), it serves Russia's strategic interests to enhance Iran's ballistic and nuclear missile capabilities.

Figure 21 shows enormous increases in Russian exports of propulsion technology, nuclear materials and guidance systems to Iran ahead of Iranian missile tests over the last three years. The fact that there is next to no trade in these sectors for most of the year and then a substantial jump in all three simultaneously before each test is indicative of Russia's intentions. For example, in January 2017 Iran carried out a missile test on the Khorramshahr ballistic missile. This liquid-fuelled missile has a heavier adapted payload of 1,800 kg and is thought to be capable of being fitted with a nuclear warhead.[197] With an estimated range of 2,000 km, it is also capable of striking key regional allies of the United States such as Israel and Saudi Arabia.

Although Iran was technically sticking to the terms of its deals, these tests inevitably attracted the ire of Donald Trump. He announced the United States would be withdrawing from the JCPOA, calling it 'a horrible one-sided deal that should have never, ever been made'. He emphasized that 'it didn't bring calm, it didn't bring peace, and it never will'.[198] To this, Ayatollah Ali Khamenei responded: 'I have directed the Atomic Energy Agency to prepare for the next steps, if necessary, to begin our own industrial enrichment without restriction.'[199]

From that moment on, tensions between the United States and Iran escalated seriously. Between May and June 2019, America moved B-52 bombers, the USS Abraham Lincoln Carrier Strike Group equipped with a Patriot missile battery, a squadron of F-22 stealth fighters and reconnaissance drones into the Gulf. National Security Advisor John R. Bolton stated that 'any attack on [US] interests or on those of our allies [would] be met with unrelenting force'.[200] The war of words between these nation's leaders also intensified: Trump threatened Iran with 'obliteration' and, following the imposition of further sanctions against Khamenei, President Hassan Rouhani referred to Trump's actions as 'mentally retarded'.[201]

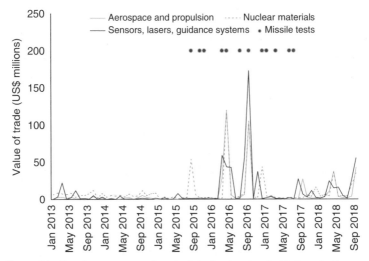

Figure 21. Russian exports of materials for Iranian ballistic missile programme, January 2013–September 2018. *Sources:* Coriolis Technologies, (dual-use goods), Foundation for Defense of Democracies (ballistic missile tests).

In this game for influence, it is Russia who is reaping the benefits. It appears that Russia may have second-guessed whether the current US administration would respond aggressively to Iranian missile tests, so it enhanced Iran's missile capabilities to nudge the situation in its favour. The fact that Iran is pursuing the objective of obtaining nuclear weapons is a situation the United States feels compelled to deal with, given that Iran is a direct threat to key US allies such as Saudi Arabia and Israel. This, again, derives from the realist, zero-sum thinking discussed in previous chapters: if your opponent uses force, victory will ensue from the use of superior force.

In addition, US withdrawal from the JCPOA has served to undermine its ability to conduct similar negotiations with North Korea over its nuclear programme. According to several sources, North Koreans are now more distrustful of the United States and its intentions to stick by the terms of any deal to which it has agreed. According to Jina Kim, a research fellow at the Korea Institute for Defense Analyses, Pyongyang was keenly focused on how the JCPOA was developing, seeing it as something of a framework for their own negotiations; however, when Trump withdrew from the deal it sent 'a clear signal to North Korea about ... [US] behaviour'. This was put even more forcefully by Tom Plant, director of the Proliferation and Nuclear Policy programme at the Royal United Services Institute: 'From the North Koreans' perspective, the Americans just can't be trusted – full stop.'[202]

What is more damaging from a US perspective – and, of course, beneficial to Russia – is that Trump's actions concerning Iran have isolated the United States from vital allies across Europe and in India. Many European leaders at the time said they 'regretted' Trump's decision, while recent speeches by EU leaders such as French president Emmanuel Macron and German chancellor Angela Merkel have revealed that

European countries may decline to enforce sanctions if Iran breaches its uranium limit under the nuclear deal.[203] Further, the implementation of a new trading system – INSTEX – that uses a barter system to allow EU-based companies to circumvent sanctions against Iran prompted Brian Hook, US Special Representative for Iran, to state: 'you can't do business with the US **and** Iran' (our emphasis).[204]

However, for Russia, it is not all about inhibiting US ascendancy: Iran is also a major factor in the equation. First, Iran is a significant military power in a strategically crucial location. It borders Iraq, Afghanistan and Pakistan, all of which harbour animosity towards US hegemony. This gives Russia the opportunity to build strong alliances across large swathes of the Middle East and Asia. Second, Iran is a major regional energy competitor in the oil and gas sector, possessing the fourth-largest proven oil reserves (roughly 158,400 million barrels). Therefore, keeping Iran isolated from the international community is to Russia's advantage. Economically, it removes a competitor; however, as we saw in the Ukrainian case study, one of the tools in Russia's trade arsenal is the use of coercive economics. If oil sanctions against Iran were to be lifted, it would severely undermine Moscow's ability to wield trade as a weapon against the EU.

Of course, there is an element of brinkmanship in this strategy: push the United States too far and it could result in war; not far enough and tensions could de-escalate. That could mean Iran is brought back into the international fold, with oil sanctions being lifted to the detriment of the Russian economy. Thus, returning to game theory, Russia's payoffs are greatest when it is striking that fine balance between peace and war: undermining US hegemony and Iran's ability to perform as a serious political or economic power in the Middle East and Central Asia while simultaneously maximizing its gains by maintaining the optimum level on all their levers of state power and achieving a geopolitical edge (see table 7).

Table 7. US–Iran power games.

		IRAN		
		Continue nuclear programme	Continue military build-up	De-escalate
US	Continue sanctions	Tensions increase (Russia wins)	Tensions increase (Russia wins)	Tensions increase (Russia wins)
	Continue military build-up	Possible war (all lose)	Possible war (all lose)	Iran loses (Russia partial loss)
	De-escalate	US loses (Russia partial loss)	Tensions increase (Russia wins)	US–Iran wins (Russia loses)

War games

By facilitating the development of Iran's missile programme, Russia can wield a great deal of influence over regional and global geopolitics without having to do that much of the legwork. By keeping tensions between the United States and Iran on a knife edge, Russia is maximizing its own utility while minimizing that of two major political and economic rivals. We have also found strong evidence that Russia can deploy strategic trade to push a state's economy to a war footing, stockpile goods to build strategic potential and furtively prop up separatist regimes through the provision of certain dual-use goods. In all cases, Russia's use of strategic trade is oblique: when an action is not accompanied by fiery rhetoric or has a limited effect on global financial markets, it tends to go unnoticed. However, strategic trade is clearly a core component of Russia's hybrid approach to warfare and its pursuit of global influence, and it warrants much closer attention. As the great World War II Soviet general Georgy Zhukov stated: 'There are things in Russia which are not as they seem.'[205]

Chapter 7

The EU: Happy Families?

In a world where the United States and Russia are playing chess (albeit interpreted differently) and China is playing *Weiqi*, it is no longer adequate for the EU to play a non-strategic game of chance. Gathering groups of nations and political allies together to build consensus was more or less effective when a liberal-democratic order assumed that everyone's shared economic interests would keep them from fighting each other. This has been the *raison d'être* of the EU since its inception. Europe needs to think strategically to address the challenges it is now facing internally and externally. Clausewitz, as we have already said, argued that war resembles a game of cards. The problem is that the EU has been playing the wrong game of cards – happy families – which is no longer viable in the current environment. It needs to shift, perhaps, to bridge, where both a strategy and an understanding of your fellow players, as well as your partner, are key to winning.

The EU was founded on the basis of two principles: to create a European Economic Area (customs union) with free trade between member states, and to move towards an 'ever closer union of peoples' in the interests of eliminating the imbalances between countries. These were seen as fundamental to avoiding war on the continent.[206] In essence, the strategy was to allow member states to thrive without internal barriers to trade and with a common external tariff on goods from outside of the union. The framework of the Treaty of Rome laid down the principles of peaceful prosperity: if countries were able to compete equally within the region, and to grow, then they would not fight each other.

These principles are coming under pressure from all sides at present. As we show in this chapter, Europe is stuck in the middle of a power struggle between Russia, China and the United States. This conflict poses a potential threat to three factors the EU has taken for granted since its inception: peace, the Western Alliance (particularly NATO) and economic strength. Similarly, and alongside this, its own unity is being threatened by populism across the region, which has been particularly evident since the migration crisis of 2015, and the strictures of its own fiscal rules, which govern the extent to which nations can control their borrowing and drive their economic growth.

Some of this was arguably inevitable. The European Economic Area delineated in the Treaty of Rome was a customs union, providing free trade for and with signatories of the Treaty and placing a common external tariff on goods coming from outside. The principles of the free movement of people, capital, goods and services were laid down in this and in the Schengen Agreement of 1985, which allowed the unimpeded passage of people without a passport between its 22 signatory nations. The Single European Act (SEA) of 1992 was the first revision of the Treaty of Rome. It created the framework within which these four 'freedoms' were integrated into the European Single Market: the European Economic Community in 1992 and the EU in 1993. The goal was to create a single market with no borders between signatory nations prohibiting the movement of people, capital, goods and services. Under the SEA, the European Parliament had greater authority, including over the principles of a common security policy.[207] The Maastricht Treaty, which created the EU, was signed in 1993. The formation of a monetary union in 1999 gave birth to the eurozone with a single currency; this was followed by the introduction of a single monetary policy in 2002. All of this brought a sense of integration and union to Europe, despite the underlying tensions and paradoxes that have ultimately led to the issues we are witnessing now, e.g. the lack of a common fiscal policy within the eurozone that would have created a transfer union as well as a monetary union under which 'richer' nations such as Germany would have supported poorer or debt-ridden ones such as Greece and Italy.

These tensions have become all too apparent. The EU's model of liberal 'social-market' capitalism was criticized by President Putin at the G20 summit in Osaka earlier this year, and the build-up of Russian troops throughout Georgia and into Ukraine has made EU member states that have borders with Russia nervous. The US administration has set its sights on reducing America's trade deficit with Europe but also questions the EU's financial commitment to Europe, as China provides a direct competitive threat. While using the language of multilateralism and integrated global supply chains, the EU has been criticized by Europe-based export credit agencies for crowding out European-funded projects due to the sheer scale of its funding and competitiveness.[208]

All of this is creating an existential challenge for Europe. Not only is the European model of capitalism under attack from all sides, and the peace on which the EU was founded growing more strained, but traditional 'nuts and bolts' engineering-based trade with a high innovation content is also under threat from digitization and, as the German's describe it, Industrie 4.0: the fourth industrial age.[209] As this chapter will show, the core strategic problem Europe is facing is that it is not, even after its moves towards ever-greater union, a bloc with any substantial strategic power. Europe is not dominant in the digital space and does not possess an independent security policy that supersedes NATO. Its internal contradictions arise from the fact that the two most powerful nations in the EU, Germany and France, agree on the principle of closer union but not on the process for getting there. While Europe appeared to assume a more confident and assertive stance immediately after the Brexit vote in 2016, this was not sustained, because the centre ground in European, and particularly German, politics has led it to become more inward looking. If Europe is to combat the current pressures being placed on its model, it needs to recover this confidence.

The pressures from without

The EU is seen as a 'mercantilist trading bloc' by the US administration.[210] What this means is that trade is being conducted by the EU in a way that promotes EU interests on EU terms. It does have a trade surplus with the United States, particularly in automotive, aerospace and machinery and components, as will be shown below. America wants to recalibrate its relationships with the EU but is not fighting the EU on its economic system in the same way that it is fighting, say, China. So, to some extent, the tug of war between Europe and the United States is not about economic systems; it is simply about trade surpluses. However, the EU has provided support to the US aerospace sector, particularly to Airbus until 2011. In April 2018 the WTO ruled that these subsidies were illegal, laying the groundwork for the United States to impose sanctions against the EU. Since then, there has been a fragile truce between the two, but there is always a risk of escalation – not least because France has imposed a 3% tax on the profits of technology companies operating in the United States, while the United Kingdom has threatened to impose a tax from April 2020. This would open up the potential for similar actions by the United States in the future.

By contrast, the challenge from China is a competitive one and affects many sectors, from rail infrastructure to digital technology. In 2016, Europe saw China as a strategic partner. Although this partnership was drawn up with terms that were in Europe's interests, the approach also had to allow China more access to partnership agreements with the EU.[211] Since then, the rejection of the merger between Siemens and Alstom in early 2019 has thrown into sharp relief the problems of scale the EU has in relation to China. The rail infrastructure projects taking place within China's borders are principally going to Chinese companies as part of the Made in China 2025 programme. While there are opportunities across the BRI, Europe's main infrastructural companies are increasingly unable to compete with Chinese firms even in their own markets and markets closer to home.[212]

Russia's strategy towards the EU has also hardened, with the country taking a more distant approach in the interests of maintaining deniability. The war in Ukraine is a major, ongoing source of tension: the Minsk Protocol in 2015[213] was intended to de-escalate the conflict in eastern Ukraine and implement a lasting ceasefire between its warring parties following Russia's annexation of Crimea in 2014. It was viewed as a statement of compromise, made within a European policy framework, as well as a measure of Europe's (particularly Germany's) strategic role and potential for global leadership. However, since then there have been daily ceasefire violations; the tabled record for March 2019 alone runs to six pages according to the Organization for Security and Co-operation in Europe's special monitoring mission in Ukraine.[214] Russia's denial of the extent of its involvement has effectively undermined the strong statement of Europe's role as leader that Merkel and Macron had hoped to present. Brexit and the Salisbury nerve agent attacks have further weakened the relationship between the EU and Russia.

The challenge from within

Europe is also facing internal challenges. The 2016 vote by the United Kingdom to leave the EU shook the latter's foundations, but predictions of its collapse proved to be premature. The union between the other member states has held strong, and there has been (as of summer 2019, at least) no dissent from the view that the United Kingdom must define the terms of its exit within the parameters set by chief negotiator Michel Barnier's Withdrawal Agreement, with no scope for renegotiation.[215] The EU, being a rules-based system, has one guiding principle when it comes to Brexit: the United Kingdom, in leaving the EU, has decided to play outside of these rules, so it must explain what it wants.

This unity is not evident elsewhere in EU policy, however. The appointment of the president and commissioner, roles that became vacant in 2019, was fraught with difficulties and suggested that Germany's role within Europe had been weakened by the candidates it chose to support, especially for the European Central Bank (ECB) governor and EU president roles. Further evidence of this weakening can be seen in broader tensions that have simmered just under the surface since the Brexit vote. These include conflicts over the fiscal stance of Italy, increased concern over the migration policy in Austria, breaches of EU values enshrined in law by Poland and Hungary, and the collapse of centrist politics in the recent European parliamentary elections.

It is this last factor that is the deepest challenge currently facing Europe, because it has economic, social and political roots. It first came to light during the migration crisis of 2015, when Germany, in the words of one senior French politician, 'broke Schengen' by allowing refugees into the country through other EU countries. Austria, Hungary and Sweden along with Germany took the most refugees, but because Greece and Italy were also key access points from Syria and North Africa, this created a humanitarian crisis and a political crisis that Europe is still coming to terms with. Germany's view was that it had a duty to take the refugees, while, as the same senior politician said at an event just before the Paris attacks in November 2015, France felt 'forced to close its border to avoid a terrorist incident'.

The populist vote in Germany goes back further than that. German political scientists have highlighted the dangers of *Rechtsextremismus* (the right-wing) since German reunification. The move by then chancellor Helmut Kohl to merge the currencies at parity, using the *Treuhand* to close the majority of eastern German businesses overnight and to finance the resultant shock to the eastern German economy via payment transfers from the western German regions, had the effect of creating anger and bitterness on both sides. Its legacy of high unemployment and lower real wages in the eastern regions has resulted in mass migration to the west by younger

Germans; those who have been left behind have reverted to populist extremes, both on the right through *Alternative für Deutschland* (AfD) and on the left through *Die Linke.*

The parallels for the rest of Europe are clear. Germany has been through a period of austerity following the assimilation of the East German regions under Helmut Kohl in the 1990s. During that time, the West German regions saw themselves as effectively subsidizing the eastern regions' economies through transfer payments that they were required to make. This has left a legacy of resentment among the electorate: the German voter does not want to see a similar 'transfer union' created in the eurozone, whereby Germany would be supporting, as they see it, the profligacy of other member states.[216] Indeed, Germany has taken a strong position against any form of fiscal union since the introduction of the euro. This means the problems of structural imbalance within Europe have been accentuated by the very element that has also triggered a trade war with the United States: Europe's (or, more accurately, Germany's) trade surplus.

All of this together has meant that both within and outside of Germany there has been a populist backlash that has kicked against the EU's structures for creating a system that embodied the ideals of convergence between nations without supplying the mechanisms to achieve them in a digital and post-financial crisis era. *The Weaponization of Trade* anticipated that Europe would take its soft consensus-based power out into the world and lead with it. The migrant crisis in Germany meant that Angela Merkel was unable to focus on the bigger European picture at the very time she needed to most. The EU's challenges since have emanated from this.

The multiplayer game

Despite these challenges, there are real reasons to be positive about Europe's future. For example, it could represent an alternative strategic game. Europe does not play chess – it has too many member states for that – and it does not play *Weiqi*, although its integrative approach should enable it to understand the players that do. Instead, Europe must show a brand of leadership now which allows it to compete in an environment that is being driven towards a power play between three different strategies. The EU's core asset is trade, and as trade is now strategic – and part of foreign policy – this should play to Europe's advantage.

Take its heavy engineering base as an example, which we shall look at through the proxy of machinery and components trading. Europe's exports to the rest of the world in this category accounted for US$1.46 trillion in 2018: that is around one-third of the total global trade in a sector that is valued at approximately US$4.4 trillion. A breakdown by country explains why Europe has the pole position in this sector. Germany, Italy, the United Kingdom and the Netherlands are the top four largest exporters in the sector, and their exports combined are worth US$698 billion; that is compared with China's US$669 billion (see figure 22).

In the current environment, size *does* appear to matter because it determines the strength of your negotiating stance. However, depth is also important. Europe's strength lies not only in the fact that it contributes such a large proportion to the total global trade in machinery and engineering, but also in its complementary sectors that work together. Heavy engineering, for example, works with electrical engineering, iron and steel, precious metals (because gold and platinum are important aspects of electronic and automotive equipment) and automotives to produce a picture of a net surplus for the EU's external trade everywhere except for China and Japan (see figure 23).

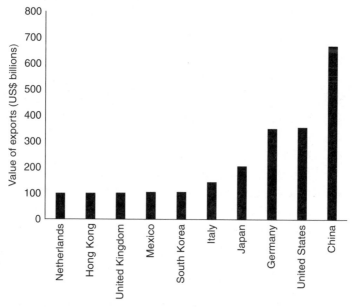

Figure 22. Top 10 countries by machinery and components sector export value, 2018 (US$ billions). *Source:* Coriolis Technologies, 2019.

It is clearly the United States and China that are the predominant trade partners in this sector, but Germany has drawn the ire of America nonetheless. Maybe this is because Germany accounts for some US$681 billion in exports from the combined engineering and automotive sectors compared with America's US$623 billion. Of the EU countries in this sector, Germany is dominant, and it is worth focusing on this to see where the problem lies. After all, when Angela Merkel starts talking about a 'strategic competition', as she did at the Munich Security Conference this year, that is a clear sign her perception of the political landscape – and the world of trade within it – has shifted.

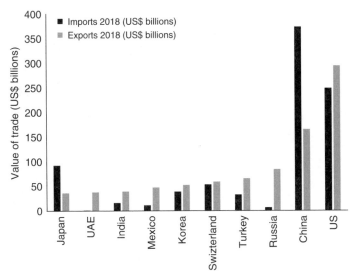

Figure 23. EU28 combined engineering and automotive sectors, imports and exports, 2018 (US$ billions). *Source:* Coriolis Technologies, 2018.

Within the engineering sector, Germany's power lies in its exports of machinery and components, and automotives. In order to fuel its supply chains, the country has a trade deficit in iron and steel, electrical equipment and precious metals (especially gold and platinum). At present, US iron and steel tariffs are being imposed on iron and steel going into the United States; however, because Germany receives its supply from within Europe, its engineering and automotive sectors are unlikely to be substantially affected by this move.

Germany's trade in the engineering sector has grown over the period 2013–2018, particularly with Spain, Poland, the United Kingdom and the United States in terms of exports, and with Poland, the United States and China in terms of imports (see figure 24).

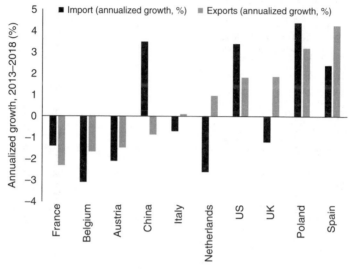

Figure 24. Germany's engineering and automotive sector supply chain (total value, annualized growth, 2013–2018 (%)). *Source:* Coriolis Technologies 2019.

What is clear is that imports *from* the United States are growing more quickly than exports to the United States across the sector, while exports to China have dropped considerably, perhaps because of the economic struggles China has been facing as a result of its trade war with the United States and general global uncertainty. In figure 24, what is perhaps more interesting is that, although trade with Poland has increased, trade with other countries within Europe has fallen. This suggests that Germany may be redistributing its supply chains within Europe and favouring eastern European nations. Poland and the Czech Republic (Germany's second-largest importer in the sector) have particularly benefited from this.

THE EU: HAPPY FAMILIES?

The engineering sector is Europe's largest combined export grouping, and Germany is its major player. The problem for Europe is that, although it has a surplus with the United States in automotives and machinery and components, the sector itself relies heavily on imports from both within Europe and, ironically, the United States and China. There is a misconception that when end (value-added) products, such as machines and automotives, have a trade surplus, this is a 'bad' thing. Because the production of final goods relies on imports of iron and steel, metals and electronics, such a misunderstanding of how trade works has the potential to undermine the success of cross-border supply chains.

Europe's engineering sector is projected to continue its steady growth of around 1.5% annually until 2022; given its size, this is substantial. Europe's strength rests in traditional manufacturing sectors: heavy engineering, automotives, pharmaceuticals and aerospace. Supply chains in these sectors are global and cross-border trade is essential. Having a high level of imports is a measure of strength rather than weakness, so, although Germany exports more cars and machinery and components than it imports, it buys more electronics and iron and steel than it sells.

This is the simple truth of comparative advantage and goes back to the basics of free trade. A country imports when it is cheaper or more effective to do that than to produce a commodity itself. Europe provides an excellent example of how this all works.

The continent is quite clearly able to compete in the traditional – literally, the 'nuts and bolts' – sectors of trade. Indeed, this is how it defines itself to a large extent: it supplies high-quality goods that are used in infrastructure and households around the world. But this is at the heart of its struggles as well. First, it has provoked the United States by trading as a bloc, which is at the core of the suspended 'dispute' between Washington and Brussels. Second, it has laid itself open to competition from China, both due to the smaller size and scale of its traditional base and due to its underinvestment in the digital and cybersecurity worlds.

The game plan

Does Europe have a game plan for creating a cohesive view around its shared values? The answer to this is a qualified yes, but, to use a sports analogy, they need to work together as a team.

The EU's difficulties cover many areas, and there are joint statements, agreements and policies to deal with all of them. Wading through its different agendas on industrial strategy and security policy is like opening a can of Alphabetti Spaghetti and may highlight the real reason the EU and its policies are experiencing a crisis of legitimacy. We are students of European security and economic/industrial policy, yet establishing any precise policies from these documents, which are diffuse and written in dense legal language, is at best an intellectual challenge and at worst an impossibility. Perhaps this is why the briefing fact sheet on Europe's Common Security and Defence Policy (CSDP) stresses the need for public accountability: 'In modern democracies, where media and public opinion are crucial to shaping policy, popular commitment is essential to sustain our commitments abroad. We deploy police, judicial experts and solders in unstable zones around the world. There is an onus on governments, parliament, and EU institutions to communicate how this contributes to security at home.'[217]

The EU's overriding foreign policy strategy is little more than an answer to Kissinger's famous question: 'Who do I call if I want to speak to Europe?' However, subsequent iterations, and most recently the establishment of the Permanent Structured Cooperation (PESCO) framework, have begun the process of defining a more distinctive European foreign policy approach.[218] This is an acknowledgement of the fact that the security landscape has changed: first because of Russia's actions in Crimea, which have made the EU members that border Baltic states edgy, and second because there is nervousness about US commitment to Europe's defence through NATO.

NATO remains the main 'underwriter' of EU defence and security policy, which is one of the United States' key areas of dispute with Europe. Trade is no less a proxy for US foreign policy in its relations with Europe than it is elsewhere. In particular, a long and strongly held view is that European nations do not contribute a sufficient amount towards defence.[219] President Trump and his Secretary of State Mike Pompeo complained about this publicly at an ill-fated G7 meeting in Canada in 2018 and at the NATO summit in 2019.

On the whole, EU countries that are also members of NATO do not contribute the full 2% of GDP that the NATO constitution requests. Estonia, Greece, Poland, Latvia, Lithuania and the United Kingdom do, however; in fact, most of these countries increased their contributions between 2017 and 2018. However, Germany contributed 1.23% of GDP in 2018 (unchanged from 2017); France, 1.82% (a slight rise from 1.78% in 2017); the Netherlands, 1.35%; Italy, 1.15%; and Spain, 0.93%.[220]

Germany's argument is that it is restricted because, under its post-war constitution, it cannot commit to an offensive military budget. The country also significantly reduced its military expenditure, particularly on personnel, during the 2000s when there seemed to be little threat to its domestic security. This holds little sway with the current US administration, which sees the reduction of Europe's trade surplus as something that can be balanced against increased contributions to NATO.

Europe's strategy acknowledges that it has lost an edge in terms of scale and digitization. Its present approach to trade agreements is to shore up its traditional strengths in manufacturing with, for example, Japan, Canada and the Mercosur countries of Latin America.[221] EU trade policy actively seeks to promote sustainability through enhancing the bloc's industry. Having a 'balanced' trade policy that covers cybersecurity, data flows, renewables, intellectual property and public procurement is key. Any foreign direct investment in these arrangements is scrutinized for security threats, and sustainable finance and supply chains are important focuses of the policy statements.

These are phrases and words that are common to many strategies, however, and might therefore be seen as 'lacking ambition'.[222] The principle on foreign direct investment flows means Europe has mechanisms for protecting itself against accusations that it is being coerced by the United States, e.g. in relation to Huawei and 5G. It also ensures that member states take a proactive approach towards intellectual property and cybersecurity. Yet, there is always a risk that the EU's policy will be subsumed under a less ambivalent one.

The case of Iranian sanctions illustrates this clearly. The EU's trade with Iran is strategically important. Europe sells cars as well as machinery, components and equipment to Iran, while Iran represents a potential source of oil and gas that would reduce the former's dependency on Russian supplies.

Europe's exports started to increase rapidly when sanctions against Iran were lifted in 2016, and major investments were made in the country by European businesses.

Nothing traded in US dollars or on US financial markets that touches Iran is allowed under America's new regime. What this means is that, if a country or company trades in US dollars with Iran, howsoever inadvertently, the United States can add impose non-compliance fines on it. The problem here is not the direct effects of sanctions on Iran. Iran as a trading partner is not that big, even though it is strategically important. Rather, it is the impact of these so-called secondary sanctions on European trade.

Recognizing the importance of this, France, Germany and Britain have put together a special purpose vehicle (SPV) to act as insurance against any fines on European businesses wanting to maintain their trading relationships with Iran. However, there are two factors that will potentially weaken this SPV before it even gets off the ground. First, businesses have not picked up on this offer of support, choosing instead to steer clear of the wrath of US regulators. Second, the US sanctions against Iran have provided SWIFT, the Belgium-based financial messaging system, with a choice: follow the US line on trade with Iran or face sanctions yourself. Unsurprisingly, in November 2018 SWIFT decided to halt its operations in Iran. Interestingly, Russia has since launched its own financial messaging system, which can be used by China, Iran, Turkey and other countries as an alternative to Western-based systems.[223] Russia has shown itself willing to participate in INSTEX,[224] as has China,[225] and this demonstrates the dilemma that Europe now faces: can it steer its own course, should it return to its traditional ally the United States or should it carve out new relationships?

Playing populist politics

Europe's problem is the erosion of trust in the centre ground. Its mainstream political parties do not have answers to the questions being raised by nationalist voters at home. The reason is simple: all policy must be built on the consensus of 28 countries. This is difficult to achieve, and, as a result, many policies, including foreign and industrial ones, come across as aspirational rather than target oriented. Further, these political parties cannot proclaim a shared 'national' interest because, by definition, that does not exist.

This conflict is inherent in European politics. While the current structure worked after the end of the Cold War, when Germany was still relatively weak, as soon as it became stronger, with a bigger trade and budget surplus, the nations within Europe complained of imbalances while the powers outside Europe complained of trade surpluses. This resulted in the collapse of the centre vote at the recent European parliamentary elections.

For all of Europe's main political parties, this parliamentary vote was supposed to be about stemming the tide of populist parties. Yet a rally in Milan the weekend before the elections brought right-wing nationalist parties from across the region together to demand changes to Europe's economic, financial and political governance. Their protests were not anti-EU as such; they were targeted directly at the European People's Party, which is a grouping within Europe of the centre-right that includes Germany's Christian Democratic Union, Ireland's Fine Gael and France's Republican Party. These protests were a push for reform, not the demise, of the EU.

In the United Kingdom, the elections were no less populist in nature, but they were dominated by Brexit and focused on delivering a clear message to Theresa May's government: one of betrayal from Brexiteers, and one of frustration from Remainers. This was a very different battle to that being waged in the rest of the EU, as the elections were not supposed to be happening and were set against a backdrop of political atrophy and sustained uncertainty for business.

We have reached this point because of the failure of both the EU and national political parties to show clear leadership following the global financial crisis as well as during its aftershocks in Greece and the eurozone. Ordinary people across the region were asked to tighten their belts and accept flat real wage growth. Meanwhile, the world's largest financial institutions – the instigators of the crisis – moved their resources to Asia and, by fuelling growth there while Europe lagged, added to the sense that an elite were benefiting while the masses were not. The effect has been a worldwide backlash against globalization, the financial structures that drove it and the political classes that supported it.

The difference in perspective between the populists who want reform in Europe and those in the United Kingdom who just want to leave it behind may be rooted in contrasting understandings of the role of trade and national interests. For the populists rallying in Milan, the EU has supported globalization by allowing the free movement of capital out of and of people in to Europe, at the expense of national control over fiscal policy. However, the problem boils down to the fact that a country's budget deficit within the eurozone has to remain at less than 3% of GDP, meaning that national governments cannot boost fiscal expenditure to mitigate flat growth.

The United Kingdom's economic populism is different because this country is not in the currency union. Many of the economic arguments for Brexit are a variation on one theme:

that it is 'impossible' to do trade deals within a customs union or the single market with a third country. However, Germany signed £17 billion worth of trade deals with China in 2018; Italy has become the first G7 country to become part of the Chinese BRI, despite reservations at the EU level; and, while these reservations were being expressed, France orchestrated aerospace and agriculture deals worth US$45 billion with China. To top it all off, the United Kingdom remains the dominant beneficiary of Chinese foreign direct investment in Europe by some distance.

So, while it is certainly the case that the United Kingdom cannot set its own external tariffs and must trade within the EU's regulatory framework while it remains under her mantle, it is absolutely not the case that UK businesses cannot form trade deals as part of the EU. Nor is it the case that those agreements cannot be supported by the national government.

Important in understanding the effects of the different premises of populism in Europe is the way in which populism itself is now realigning trade policy globally. This has become particularly marked in the past three years as the United States has taken an overtly nationalist approach towards trade with the rest of the world, and with China in particular.

The United States has taken a nearly identical stance towards China, Japan, the EU and the United Kingdom in its trade negotiations. It will promote its own security, its own technology, its own agriculture and manufacturing, and its own currency above all other interests. Trade has become a tool of its coercive foreign policy. The case of Huawei illustrates that America is seeking to achieve its own national security objectives by influencing the trade of others, in this case the EU and the United Kingdom. In contrast, the core economic issue in the eurozone has been the same since its inception: an over-reliance on austerity and monetary policy at the level of the ECB that has failed to address the concerns of voters on the ground, first in Greece and now in Italy.

The case of Brexit: which one is trumps?

As the United Kingdom went to the European polls, the manifest and complex issues of trade, globalization, political failure and UK identity outside of the EU were subsumed into a protest on the failings of its government to negotiate Brexit. The rhetoric was that of independence at all costs, but in a world where political influence is driven by the leverage extractable from the size of a country's trade, the key question is whether or not the United Kingdom can survive alone.

The United Kingdom is responsible for 2.5% of world trade, a figure that represents a drop in 2010, immediately after the financial crisis, of just under 5%. This is in line with similar declines in the share of world trade in France, Germany, Italy and the United States, which have all seen their portion recede as China's has increased. However, there are two reasons to be concerned about the United Kingdom's position in trade terms.

First, UK trade is strategic and heavily concentrated in five key sectors outside of oil (see figure 25). Machinery and components, automotives, pharmaceuticals, electrical engineering and aerospace are all sectors considered to be 'dual use' in that a large proportion of the products they cover have both civilian and military purposes. The proportion of UK trade that is dual use, i.e. strategic, is 30%, and 60% of UK trade with the EU is in these sectors. What this means is that if the United Kingdom becomes detached from these supply chains, it will be isolated in defence sector terms specifically.

The EU emphasizes the research and development elements of defence and security in its strategy documents, focusing on big science projects such as the European satellite programme, Galileo. In leaving the EU, the United Kingdom will be excluding itself from large-scale and collaborative projects directly related to defence and security, which is a serious consideration regarding its future security capabilities.

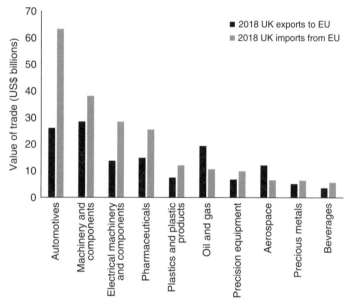

Figure 25. Top 10 sectors for UK trade with the EU, 2018 (US$ billions). *Source:* Coriolis Technologies, 2019.

Second, this figure of 2.5% of world trade is a concern quite simply because of the United Kingdom's size. The EU has, as already discussed, signed trade arrangements since the United Kingdom voted to leave with Canada, Japan and the Mercosur countries. Together, these deals give European companies free trade access to over 42% of world trade; negotiations with the United States are still under discussion.

This year, early June was dominated by the state visit of President Trump to the United Kingdom. The timing could not have been worse. The president brought his zero-sum negotiating style to a UK government that existed in name only and had no vision for what its relations would be with the United States, whether in the short, medium or long term. Nor, indeed, did it have a clear view of what its relations would be with *itself* immediately after Trump's visit.

This visit was not really about trade, or Brexit, or who was to lead the UK Conservative Party. It was the visit of a president who has uniquely used his position to begin the process of redefining America's relationships with the rest of the world on its own terms. Unlike the United Kingdom, President Trump and the US administration have an unambiguously clear view of what they want: to Make America Great Again.

While we were writing this book, US trade negotiators and officials made it clear to us that they believe the United Kingdom should use Brexit as an opportunity to strike trade deals with the United States. They also explained that the United Kingdom will have to accept not only US standards in agriculture and food safety but also US investment in UK public services. Other priorities of the United States include fair market access for its manufacturers and the maintenance of a favourable value for the US dollar against the pound sterling. There will be no special arrangements for the United Kingdom.

It is evident, then, that the United Kingdom will be the weaker partner in any negotiations it undertakes at the moment. It has a mild goods deficit with the United States, but its exports in cars, pharmaceuticals and aerospace have all increased over the past five years by, respectively, 12%, 4% and 1.5%. Given the sensitivity of the United States to these sectors – particularly automotives – the United Kingdom, whether or not it is part of the EU, could well fall victim to US tariffs imposed on origin grounds, since it imports roughly 48% of the value it exports in this sector.

The United States is set on influencing the policies of its allies. The United Kingdom's approach to 5G and Huawei has been called into question by the US administration in relation to the Five Eyes security collaboration (which includes the United States, Australia, New Zealand, Canada and the United Kingdom). It has been suggested that if the United Kingdom uses Huawei for these contracts it may jeopardize its position within that network.

The United Kingdom does not represent a national security threat to the United States: its trade is too small and in deficit anyway. It contributes at least the minimum threshold of 2% of GDP to NATO and is therefore not on the naughty step regarding that either. The problem is that the United Kingdom is an open economy, and highly dependent on imports. Any trade deal will reflect this: the United Kingdom will be a price taker outside of the EU, not a deal maker.

Strategy the European way

The EU carries the lessons of history as it formulates its strategies. The fact that it behaves as one 'country' in trade and, in the case of the eurozone, financially means it *is* what it set out to be in the Treaty of Rome: a means of preventing war in Europe through economic union. This is in its DNA. However, it is not a nation but a trading bloc. Accordingly, every member state has different cultures that underpin their approaches to Europe and their attitudes towards shared European strategies in defence and security.

This is a strength as well as a weakness. The EU's consensus approach means that its primary objective – avoiding war among member states – has been achieved. It renders the strategic game a team, or at least a partner, activity, and it makes compromise the most likely outcome. In areas such as the environment as well as threats from non-state actors and hackers, this may be a good thing. It remains to be seen how consensus-based politics will fare against the direct strategies being implemented at present by Russia, China and the United States. Europe's dilemma for the next decade at least will be whether to become more strategic and integrated as a bloc, or whether to allow its nations to function individually. This dilemma is as old as Europe itself, but as times change it becomes an increasingly important one to consider.

Chapter 8

The playbook: strategy in action

This book is unapologetically theoretical at times, and there is a reason for this. We know that games are all about strategy and that strategy is all about outcomes. In order to get a desired outcome, you need a theory, or a framework, around which to build your strategy. Theory is not a bad thing, nor is it technical or dull: it informs us what we should do next. This chapter is all about what our next move should be based on the theory of the world we have constructed.

First, let us summarize our theory. We have argued that trade is being gamed: of the strategic choices open to states, trade is regarded as a versatile weapon that can be wielded in the quest for power and influence. Thus, in the modern era, it is being used as a proxy for the larger battle that is being fought between the world's most powerful nations and trading blocs. A struggle that was primarily about physical, territorial hegemony is now also about supremacy over the digitalized paradigm that has emerged from the post-Cold War era and the global financial crisis.

So, why is trade so important, given that it is all about geopolitics – that is, control over borders, resources, risks and financial flows – which has dominated global interactions these past 200 years or more? Surely this is an old battleground, one with which we are all familiar and that can be articulated clearly within an increasingly nationalist rhetoric because it speaks of zero sums: of winning while your rival loses. In fact, it is *precisely* this that makes trade excellent grounds on which to fight, because the world knows its rules. However, a new game and new rules are being made up as this battle rages on, due to the power struggle for control of digitalization and data.

Our central theme is that, while it may be true that we are becoming increasingly embroiled in an old-fashioned trade war, this is a distraction from what is really going on. The definition of power has shifted from geopolitics, based on the interplay of military and economic strength, to *paradigmatic politics: paradigmatic power.* This paradigm is based on the power of the cloud and cyberspace. It is less about the control of land and resources and more about the control of networks that drive the cross-border flows of information, finance and intellectual property. It is all about the control of data and data flows.

We do not argue that control for physical space is no longer relevant – far from it. Indeed, much of Russia's strategic approach is dedicated to the reclamation and restoration of territory it lost following the Cold War. Further, Russia holds genuine concerns over EU and NATO encroachment into its 'spheres of influence'. Thus, the competition for resources, territory and classic geopolitics will remain an essential component of state strategies.

Instead, we propound that we are entering a new paradigm (a 'techno-economic paradigm' as it is known in the evolutionary economics world). We view what is happening as a paradigm shift because it possesses distinctive features that are changing the way we work, the way we live, the way we do business and the way in which we see politics. The everyday existence of the ordinary person is split between the virtual world – through social media and their online identity, where they have power and influence – and the real world, where their control and their input are limited. This has created the populism that has enabled the language of economic nationalism. As Putin pointed out at the G20 meeting in Osaka in 2019, this could be seen as the failure of liberalism *and* the failure of convergence.

The world is moving on to something new, and, in that transition, we are seeing a resurgence of the nation state, neo-liberalism and neo-realism, where power is, once again, everything. While power has always been important, during the era of convergence that power was diverted from nations to businesses. Meanwhile, digitization and rapid technological integration have allowed nations to influence people and democracies, not just through culture or the military but also through what the National Endowment for Democracy calls 'sharp power': coercive influence through education and media of authoritarian regimes.[226] As we move between paradigms towards the control of both physical and digital space, this becomes nothing other than paradigmatic power.

This paradigmatic politics is profoundly different to geopolitics. In it, trade is strategic: it is the fulcrum of foreign policy because it is a familiar instrument of belligerence and allows countries to compete for the upper hand using, in Roosevelt's words, 'all means short of war'.[227] What we are seeing is a 'high stakes peacetime competition with all red lines blurred, if not erased'.[228] This is a world of 'weaponized interdependence', where even though the great powers want to avoid a major war, their strategies are no less militaristic and no less coercive in both theory and action. Here, trade data, imports and exports, logistics and transactions flows, and company behaviours within nation's supply chains are the mechanisms through which winning or losing is measured. Having control of that information is everything.

Many have argued that it is this interdependence in the digital space that has created the need for our current power struggle.[229] In contrast, our theory is that this interdependence is bigger than the digital space, if that is possible. While control of the digital world order is a prerequisite and the ultimate end game, it is trade that links the 'old' world order with this new paradigm. It makes this struggle visible to ordinary people and politicians. In short, it is a 'known' foreign policy and an ideal proxy for the real conflict that none of us can see.

Trade wars as we are seeing them are apparently being waged in the familiar space of tariffs and retaliation, where winning or losing is obvious. They are not literally violent; thus, we need to use the word 'war' with some caution, as discussed in chapter 3. They are, however, political and aggressive, and they contain many of the features of war, such as coercion tactics to influence competitors and allies as well as aggression, retaliation and strategic moves from individual countries. We would argue that it is the coercive elements of trade wars that can be won. Imposing a tariff on a country makes it change its behaviours: the reduction in Chinese exports to the United States in sectors targeted by tariffs is an example of this. China has curtailed its exports to the United States, so the latter – on paper, at least – has 'won'. However, as we have pointed out, the fact that China has started its 'long march' to technological independence means that, in a longer-term game, victory for the United States cannot be assured by any means. America's mode of retaliation – taking action against businesses and countries who operate with Chinese technologies, particularly in the 5G and security areas – is an attempt to display its control over the current paradigm.

The fact that this can only function as a short-term response, however, highlights the differences in the way paradigmatic power is being fought over via trade 'games'. The United States has a direct, coercive strategy. This is best articulated as a 'winner takes all' approach: winning is non-negotiable and done using quick-fire tactics without the appearance of a long-term objective. As a result, the US strategy has the appearance of being unplanned, irrational and ultimately damaging to the country and its role as unilateral global policeman, which it adopted after the fall of the Berlin Wall.

Yet our chapter on US strategy demonstrated that this approach is entirely rational and chess-like in its precision. Any threats to national security are clearly identified as targets: the revisionist states of China and Russia are to be tackled through economic and technological as well as more conventional means. The rogue states, such as Iran and North Korea, are to be similarly targeted through sanctions and trade finance restrictions, rather than through bombs and battles. Unconventional, non-state threats such as terrorism and hackers are to be fought through research and development, particularly on data and military security. Finally, the domestic threat of immigration control is to be dealt with through tariffs and trade agreements.

All of this is under the guise of reducing the US budget deficit. Why? Because China and other foreign powers, including Japan and the EU, own sufficiently large portions of this deficit – that is, of US debt – to be able to exercise disproportionate influence over the United States and, indeed, the global economy, should they decide to sell it all in one go.

The US dollar's hegemony is everything in the global trading system, and its weakness is the US deficit. While America can, and does, prevent access to financial markets and US dollar trading, this hegemony is only guaranteed in the short term. However, conflict in the trade finance space, as we have suggested, is the economic equivalent of pushing the nuclear button: it is a last resort. That is why trade war conversations are currently at a stalemate that could last for years.

In contrast, China has an integrated and 'global' strategy that it has packaged up as multilateral and collaborative. In the words of a senior politician at a London-based event in 2019: 'We have a big surplus, and we want to use that surplus to help other countries to grow in the same way that we have.' This is the Chinese definition of multilateralism, embodied through the BRI. The projects being funded through this initiative are, as was highlighted, predominantly about energy and infrastructure: the BRI has arguably been set in motion to build a system along China's key trade routes, which rivals the Western definition of liberalism and convergence. While it suited the Chinese agenda to work with Western powers for the 30 years after the end of the Cold War, there was always some concern about undue US influence, and this has come to light under Xi Jinping's growth-oriented strategy. Having power and influence are China's historical right according to Xi, and Made in China 2025, along with all the resources that are being assigned to it, is simply a mechanism for restoring the country to its former glory.

This is different to the United States' winner takes all game. Chinese power is entirely strategic and can be called 'soft' in that it is economic and technological rather than political. It is difficult to argue that China is imposing its political system on other countries; it certainly does not see its approach as being one of dominance, politically or militarily, even if data on its levels of military spending would suggest otherwise. China is playing a long-term game. As in the traditional strategy game *Weiqi*, the country does not need to fight, and it does not necessarily need to win; it just needs to dominate.

Russia has taken yet another approach, because it has neither the hard power of the United States nor the soft power of China. It cannot 'win' on economic terms. It is a commodity-based economy, and its financial influence is based on the wealth this creates. In terms of trade, its influence is minimal except in the energy sector. However, Russia has two areas of influence that will always justify its having a seat at the table. While it learnt the rules of the convergence game during the post-Cold War period, it also built up resentment at the unilateral power assumed by the United States. Russia has lengthened its military reach since the collapse of the Soviet Union to ensure that it retains influence in the strategic parts of its former empire and beyond.

Russia's interpretation of strategic trade is arguably the most creative of the great powers. It has taken steps to protect its own interests and augment its capabilities in Ukraine through the provision and stockpiling of dual-use goods. Over in Syria, its strategy has been driven in part by the objective of expanding its naval capabilities in order to pose a threat to Europe from the Mediterranean, the Black Sea and the North Sea. However, Russia's wider strategy in the Middle East has also been about riling the United States and undermining its hegemony. Russia has built relations with Iran, with China through the BRI, and it is also bolstering its strategic influence in countries such as Saudi Arabia and the UAE. It offered support to Qatar during a blockade by Saudi Arabia, Bahrain, the UAE and Egypt, erected in protest of the country's apparent support for terrorism. Russia provided alternative trade routes to Qatar, thereby undermining the potential for coercion, if that was the blockade's intention. Similarly, it has provided strategic goods so that Syria and Iran may counteract the effects of sanctions. Russia has also helped to enhance Iran's ballistic missile programme in order to frustrate the United States and keep Iran isolated. Its newest approach – developing alternative financial mechanisms for trading with Iran – allows it to explicitly and directly contravene US policy.

As with the trade war between China and the United States, there is an element of misdirection in the conflict between America and Russia. Make no mistake, Russia wants power and influence, and its burgeoning relationship with China is simply a 'marriage of convenience': there is no love lost between these two countries. But as the United States becomes more and more isolationist – withdrawing from the Middle East, taking a more arms-length approach to NATO and the defence of Europe, and using trade rather than military means to fight its battles – this is giving Russia the opportunity to build in areas where it really wants to assume power: specifically, cyberspace.

Europe, then, is stuck in the middle of a power struggle for a new era, which has data, information, intellectual property and cybersecurity at its heart. As a collection of nations, a myopic game plan and a sense of 'winning' will never be part of its approach to the strategic competition in which we now find ourselves: this is a far cry from the consensual political model on which the EU was based, with its focus on the collective interest. Europe's approach is to manage different strategic perspectives and come to a compromise. This does not mean that its nations, businesses or even its politicians do not want to compete. Rather, it means they want to find the best way of optimizing the potential of European research and development, innovation, business and growth to secure the most stable environment for the largest number of people across the region.

The big difference between the United States, China, Russia and Europe is that the latter cannot seek power because of the way it is constituted. It does not have the status of a nation; therefore, although the EU can talk about the ways in which its citizens, businesses and member states might perform better, be more environmentally friendly and sustainable, and act more inclusively, it cannot tell them exactly how to do this. It is an enabling organization rather than a coercive one: historically, it has not played competitive games itself but has helped others to take part.

This approach is unsustainable on several levels. The United States sees the EU as a competitor, not only because of its trade surplus but also because its defence is subsumed into NATO, and therefore US and European security are inextricably linked. Russia also sees the EU's collectiveness as something to be challenged, while China sees European businesses and banks as potential partners – on Chinese terms, of course – in the BRI and in the EU itself. Europe has become a part of the global struggle, and it urgently needs the tools to adapt and reassert its influence.

As we have seen, both Europe's strategic position globally and its own cohesion are at stake. It is not immune to the tide of populism, either: as discussed, this tide, coming from both the left and the right, swept away the centrist parties at the 2019 European elections. It does have strategies to build consensus around defence, and potentially to build a defence force through PESCO. In addition, the European Commission is aware that building its legitimacy with voters across the region is vital. We argued that Brexit was a symptom rather than the cause of Europe's problems, and its unified approach to Brexit has shown that it is capable of taking a direct, perhaps even a winner takes all, approach to problems that may affect its future cohesion.

If this is the game, what is the plan?

The threats of the new paradigm are clear. Every strategic case – the United States, China, Russia and Europe – lists more or less the same areas of risk: cyberattacks; intellectual property development and protection; trade and competitiveness; the preservation of old sectors and the promotion of new ones; and non-state actors, e.g. terrorists or hackers, who can kill or damage systems as much as they can nations. There are also broader issues, such as digital identity, data ownership and control, and personal security, both in an economic and a well-being sense, which are underpinning the rise of populism. However, overriding everything at both the political and the populist levels is a sense of urgency against a backdrop of confusion. The stark national strategies we are seeing now are a response to all of this.

It is not our intention to criticize any of these national strategies: each is based on culturally specific value systems and social norms that have evolved with the histories of the countries employing them. These strategies reflect both the strengths and the weaknesses of such values. We simply want to point out that the world's great powers are playing a dangerous game of chicken with one another. This tit-for-tat retaliation, in trade, technology and diplomatic terms, has defined the foreign policy framework since 2016 – when

Trump came into power – but it arguably has earlier origins. It seems no country is to blame, but no country is entirely innocent either.

However, 'we are where we are' is the problem, not the solution. If the world is becoming more competitive as its major powers seek to dominate the new paradigm, then we are likely to see greater confusion and considerable uncertainty in the immediate, and even the long-term, future. We have reached an impasse in trade terms, where the big players cannot escalate the situation much further because the consequences would be too bad: the global financial system might collapse, and we might end up with two parallel internet/digital systems that operate under different political regimes, one for the East and one for the West.

The solution, then, is not a national but a multilateral strategy. In short, we all need to be playing a multiplayer game like the EU. The threats we are facing are common to all, and the biggest one – barely covered in any of the national strategies except for Europe's – is the climate crisis, which is threatening our very existence. It is extraordinary that, at a time when the world's sustainability, trade systems, economy, environment and security are being threatened by non-state and global factors, we are even *thinking* about nationalism. It is a measure of the powerlessness of consensus politics to interpret popular opinion that we are in this position. The sad fact is that we are, however, and any current strategy must give multilateral and international organizations and businesses the power to recapture the lost ground of legitimacy.[230] The international rules-based system and its institutions need to work with corporates and the finance sector to adapt, reform and create strategies that align national with international interests. Europe has a responsibility to look out rather than in and to lead the way.

Strategy for trade professionals in business and banking

We believe that these are steps that can be taken by businesses as much as by international institutions. As we argued earlier, the banking and finance sectors are to some extent responsible for the position we are now in. Their unquestioning support of global economic growth and convergence meant that a trail of 'have nots' were left behind after the financial crisis, and these are the same people who are voting for neo-liberal, nationalist politicians now. Any remedy must go beyond 'making people love banks'. This is never going to happen. However, businesses and financial institutions can show some initiative in two key areas.

First, they must acknowledge their part in creating the present situation. Most of the banking professionals and business leaders with whom we spoke while writing this book agree: politicians are wielding tools to gain power that will ultimately do damage if they carry on using them. By supplying more data to governments and multilateral organizations, and by being more transparent about how trade and trade finance actually work, financial institutions can help them to correct policies and formulate effective strategies. If nothing else, a separation of trade finance transactions systems along East–West lines or, indeed, a trade war leading to the collapse of the financial system are not in the interests of either businesses or banks. Being more open about the arms and dual-use goods trades as well as supply chain transactions, at least in terms of data, has to be a core part of the leadership role this sector takes on. It is no longer enough to sit on the sidelines and complain about politicians.

Bringing this idea of transparency to the level of businesses and their relationships with clients, the former must inform the public about the security risks attached to data. Just who owns our data and who is responsible for protecting it are the key challenges of our time. In the current, unregulated environment, it is the responsibility of those who acquire and hold data to explain how that data is being used and, more importantly, how it is being kept safe. This may seem trivial in relation to the power struggles between nations we have been discussing, but 'sharp' power – the power to influence and coerce through control of communications and data – is entirely dependent on gaining access to that data in the first place. Around 2.41 billion people worldwide trust Facebook with information about themselves: their likes and dislikes, their family connections and even their daily routines.[231] Once you are a Facebook user, or indeed a Google or a Twitter user, you can log into other platforms using the same details. Anyone wanting to accumulate information about you can simply 'screen scrape' your digital footprint. Your identity and privacy can now be easily profiled and just as easily weaponized. Our businesses and financial institutions have a responsibility to promote open automated platform interfaces (APIs), which, compared with screen scraping, are more secure and, more importantly, leave control of data with the individual user.

Multilateral strategy

Below, we identify five key areas that we believe any international game plan should deal with as clearly and methodically as the US national strategy deals with threats (actual or perceived) to its system. It is no longer viable for the centre ground in business and politics to wait for the current global climate of uncertainty to subside: this is not going to happen anytime soon, and, in the interim, these dangers will accumulate.

1. Play by the rules

When it comes to data, regulation and standardization must be the first port of call in any international strategy. Within the digital paradigm, data is important as a source of competitive advantage in business, finance and politics alike. Knowing something your competitor does not is essential when you are playing an asymmetric game: it gives you first-mover advantage.

The risks here are obvious. Large amounts of data go into the cloud and can be used to manipulate opinions, accumulate power and undermine political systems, all beyond the control or say-so of the people who actually own it, i.e. voters and buyers. At a transactional level, this, in the words of a senior banker, creates 'digital islands'. As these islands develop separately, there is a risk that each has different standards, which increases complexity and the scope for fraud and crime.

Alongside this, we are seeing an increased interest in cryptocurrencies. As Martin Wolf points out, Facebook's plan to launch a cryptocurrency named Libra has been simultaneously welcomed as a move towards financial inclusion and railed against as a step too far. [232] The danger is that, unregulated, individuals will be able to store debt in tokens they cannot recoup to pay debts or to hide financial fraud in blockchains beyond the reach of orthodox detection systems.

It is not our purpose to debate the rights and wrongs of this move. However, since the financial crisis, banks have put a large amount of effort into tightening their own AML, KYC and compliance rule books as well as ensuring that default and credit risks are as low as possible in the trade finance and transactions banking sectors. The problem is that there is a yawning gap of US$1.5 trillion in the amount of trade finance required by SME exporters that current financial systems cannot provide.[233] Similarly, on the consumer side, there are around 1.7 billion people in the world who do not have a bank account according to the World Bank (cited in *Forbes*).[234]

This market is too big, and the scope of cryptocurrencies is too extensive for it not to be a rich seam of competitiveness in the future. Indeed, at a recent Sibos event, one senior banker was asked if they could imagine a world in which cryptocurrencies were used to do business in sanctioned countries beyond the watchful eye of US regulators. Their answer was an unequivocal yes.

Banks are being disintermediated, not by the fintechs with whom they largely work in a collaborative way, but by 'big tech'. Much of the work they have done to minimize the risk of unethical or unsustainable supply chains and unreliable credit, to improve trustworthiness checks and to lessen unaffordability will be undone if the emerging technology companies are not regulated. The danger, of course, is that Google, Amazon, Facebook and Microsoft may soon be playing a different technology game to Alipay, Tencent and Alibaba.

2. Stop playing monopoly

The risks now stem from the fact that the world's economic system is reliant on the US dollar. This gives the United

States a disproportionate capacity to shut this system down if it feels that is a strategic move worth making. We have highlighted the risks of this approach in terms of US debt sales by Japan, China and even the EU and argue that, even though the power to control financial networks belongs to the United States and the power to collapse the global economy belongs to China, this 'nuclear option' is unlikely to be used. The trade war has reached its own deterrent equilibrium.

However, granting the US dollar hegemony is not a positive move. Yet alternative reserve currencies such as the yen and the euro are either insufficiently important within the trade system or too underdeveloped to have taken this role. As Wolfgang Münchau points out, the word 'euro' is associated with the word 'crisis', and this has not helped its standing in global markets or indeed trade.[235] He goes on to say that currencies have become geopolitical. We would argue that they have become paradigmatic, not least because of their potential, as discussed above, to become digital.

What this means is that the ECB and eurozone member states have to take a leadership role with business to promote the euro as an alternative to the 'exorbitant privilege', as Münchau calls it, of US dollar hegemony. This campaign may be spearheaded by Europe's banks and businesses themselves, of course: setting prices in euros rather than in US dollars is an uncomplicated mechanism for doing this, and while the complexities of secondary sanctions would not dissipate as a result, this move would at least begin to recalibrate the financial rules of world trade around a European framework.

3. Play fair in free trade

Ironically, 'balanced' and 'fair' free trade is something on which all national strategies agree. The WTO is weak at the moment; it must do more to justify its existence by demonstrating that it understands both the nature of free trade and its consequences. In essence, it has to 'take the game' to the United States and China, who are both breaking the rules at present. Europe, in the interest of consensus, has filed complaints against both countries, but the United States has declared the dispute resolution systems are not fair and has made national security claims against them. The US approach is to undermine the judges who resolve those disputes by not replacing them. China's approach is to claim multilateralism and adhere to this WTO rules-based era. However, the perceived threat of intellectual property theft, the role of state-funded programmes and the restrictions around foreign investment mean that US and EU grievances cannot be ignored. Nevertheless, the dispute resolution system will be defunct by the end of 2019, leaving the WTO at the whim of national strategy right when it needs to be most vocal.

This is unsustainable. To reiterate, globalization is not trade, although trade is the means through which the digital era of globalization – the paradigm shift – is being contested by the big powers. The cause of this is twofold. First, there are obvious reasons why the world trade system has produced national grievances and will continue to do so. Countries have not 'played nice' and the result is a system that is, at present, irretrievably damaged. Unless it can reform and incorporate the new digital reality of trade quickly, the dispute between China and the United States – and the United

States and its other trading partners – will signal its demise. It is impractical to call for reform. Rather, we are calling for an urgent recalibration of the WTO to direct its work towards understanding the nature of the current trade conflict and building a strategy accordingly. A working party on digitization, however interesting, simply will not address the need for action now.

The current system also requires governments and export credit agencies to understand the competitive landscape of trade and the role of governments within that. Up to now, this has been governed by the OECD Consensus, an agreement on the principles of export credits to help nationally important exporting businesses gain these for their activities. Tightening up the OECD Consensus is vital, as there are signs it is fragmenting: China's export credit agencies are now able to finance proportionately more companies, while the United States has until recently taken a more arms-length and market-based approach to supporting its EXIM. This has left the EXIM without a full mandate, which is unfair in a world that is becoming increasingly nationalistic. The renewal of its mandate is welcome, as will be the renewal of its charter in September 2019; but the role of governments in supporting strategically important trade must be done within international frameworks to ensure that the playing field is level.

Second, and perhaps more importantly, the political, business and economic actors who have benefited from world trade throughout history have not explained why trade matters to people who have been disadvantaged by the era of globalization and convergence. This has created populism and a backlash against trade. Trade creates jobs, innovation and competitive dynamism in a world where technology makes the relationships between peoples, cultures and opportunities symbiotic rather than competitive.

This is a complex but positive message that it is our duty to articulate. Trade has fuelled the world since the ancient days of the Phoenicians, Persians, Romans and the old Silk Road. There have always been winners and losers; but an interdependent postmodern world does not tolerate that. We are where we are because of a lack of leadership. This is a responsibility that should equally belong to Europe, as this bloc represents a shared interest in a multilateral approach to trade.

4. Save the planet

It is impossible to overstate the magnitude of the current environmental crisis. While our book is not about that, it should be noted that trade is not benign from an environmental point of view. The industry is well aware that large ships pollute more than automobiles or aeroplanes and are damaging the environment.[236] Unfortunately, moving trade into the digital space does not help much: people will always need products that come from around the world. Nor are blockchains an environmentally sustainable solution: the hardware that supports bitcoin, for example, uses 66.7 terawatt-hours of electricity per year, which is comparable to the total energy consumption of the Czech Republic and is a greater amount than 159 countries around the world.[237]

Trade has to clean up its act. The ICC Banking Commission has turned its attentions towards developing common regulatory standards for the industry,[238] while a number of standards have emerged that require banks to report on sustainable trade finance and sustainable supply chains.

187

These are governed by compliance as well as KYC and AML considerations.

The environment is not a source of competitive advantage, but it represents a shared problem for the world that is not going away anytime soon. Tackling environmental degradation is one of the drivers behind China's approach to long-term competitiveness and industrial policy, and its key strength. If we do not act, the consequences for everyone will be dire. We believe national and supranational organizations must ensure the environment is considered in every area of industry, trade and competitiveness strategy. While this is certainly the case in Europe and China, it is not evident in US strategy. The United States urgently needs to be a part of these environmental discussions again, because its absence is, quite literally, unsustainable.

5. Understand populism

Finally, the world has a shared problem in populism. This is the vicious cycle we referred to in chapter 1. The slowing of growth and trade has created a sense of exclusion among those who have not benefited from the upsides of the globalization era. This has created a populist backlash that politicians have sought to address through a nationalist language centred around trade. This is compelling and easy to understand. However, it generates protectionism and barriers to trade that, as we have begun to see in 2019, creates business uncertainty and slows growth further.

Until we break this cycle, the world's uncertainties around trade and the trade war will not abate. We know businesses, banks and governments can do more to promote sustainable development goals and monitor their supply chains to ensure sound ethical and sustainable practices are in place. Economic growth is as important as a sense of economic well-being, and the critique of Western liberalism is that its constant focus on economic growth means it will always perpetuate inequality and social exclusion.

This is a trade problem because, as we have said numerous times, trade is acting as a proxy for the real power struggle raging on between the biggest powers at present. That struggle has become marked because of the rise of populist politics and therefore cannot be ignored. Any new strategy must promote the interests of the people and champion their right to control their own data and, by extension, their lives.

Game over

The trigger for this book was the trade war between China and the United States. In game theory terms, we are convinced that the outcome will be a 'satisficing' one, where neither side loses and both sides can be seen to have 'won' against their own values (see table 8).

The only circumstances under which the international community wins is if both China and the United States de-escalate. This is not in America's best interests, because, strategically, it is not supportive of the WTO in its current format and such a move would run the risk of China escalating. However, it *is* in China's interests to de-escalate or compromise, not least because it sees itself – rhetorically, at least – as a supporter of the WTO and as a country that wants to avoid conflict.

The most likely outcome is that both sides will come to a compromise. This does not mean there is no role for the international community to play. Indeed, the international community needs to provide the strategy 'bridge' that will transport us to the next paradigm, through regulation and standardization, free trade, counterbalances to US dollar hegemony, mechanisms to incorporate sustainability into supply chains and support for those who have been excluded from the process of globalization.

Table 8. A stylized game theory outcome
for the US–China trade dispute.

		US		
		Escalate	Compromise	De-escalate
CHINA	Escalate	No one wins – economic equivalent of pushing nuclear button – financial crisis	China can hail win but there is an unstable truce	China wins
	Compromise	US can hail win but there is an unstable truce	Both sides win against own value system	China wins
	De-escalate	US wins	US wins	International organizations, like WTO, win

The game at present is not about trade, economic or military power alone; it is about hegemony, and the international community must be equally aware of this. A messy battle between Russia, China and the United States is on the horizon, and Europe may struggle to secure its identity in the new world order. In terms of Brexit, the United Kingdom has a strategic choice to make: turn to the United States (because that is where power and influence seemingly lie in the digital era) or turn to Europe (because that is where the United Kingdom's values intrinsically rest). What is absolutely clear is that the United Kingdom cannot survive by itself.

Two years ago, in our book *The Weaponization of Trade*, we pointed out that if the world continued along nationalistic and isolationist lines, the global trading system would disintegrate. We stated that the risks of trade war leading to military war could not be excluded because of miscalculation, and this remains the case. We urged politicians to show humility and step back from their entrenched positions.

Two years ago, we were already too late. The recent popularization of the phrase 'trade weaponization' has served only to create a sense in the centre ground that there is no hope for a moderate, business-and-people-led agenda that works with rather than against trade partners. The United States sees trade competition as positive between allies; we have yet to see evidence that this is the case.

All business leaders and centre-ground politicians reading this text need to acknowledge that we are past the point of no return: we are living in a world where big powers fight for hegemony of the world order. However, this world order has changed, as have the means of controlling it.

We have offered some practical, trade-based suggestions to pull this industry back from the brink; but these suggestions will not steer us smoothly towards the new paradigm. The challenge strategists are facing is that they must revisit the framework of foreign policy: do we want to see a world in which neo-realist approaches among our great powers dominate – a world where power, influence and self-interest are everything? Among the business and banking communities we have worked with, the answer is a resounding 'absolutely not'. Multilateralism – common threats addressed in a shared way through international action – is the route that most want to take.

The alternative is an endgame that is too calamitous to contemplate.

Acknowledgements

To paraphrase Oscar Wilde: 'To write one book with a parent may be regarded as a misfortune; to write two looks like carelessness.'

As a mother-and-son team, we are unusual in that we are indebted to the same people for their constancy, support and patience while we have been working on this book. We apologize for the dinner table conversations we've monopolized, the wedding preparations we've ignored, the dishes we haven't washed and the shopping we haven't done. Dennis and Gaini, Charlie and Laura: we love you, and we thank you. We owe you a pint of Harvey's, at least.

No book is the work of one person, or indeed of two, and we are eternally grateful to Professor Beatrice Heuser for her support and guidance; to Hiroshi Nakatani, who has patiently endured missed deadlines; to Jack Davies, whose inspirational insight into sharp power came just at the right moment; and to our colleagues at Coriolis Technologies, who have made sure that the wheels stay on the business while we write. Pete Murray, Adam Taylor and Iain Anderson from Cicero as well as Kate McAndrew and Ben Wright kept us cheerful. They reminded us about the important things in life – like wine and football, and not taking yourself too seriously – when they would have been easy to forget. GTR's Ed Virtue,

ACKNOWLEDGEMENTS

Pete Gubbins and Shannon Manders made sure we kept on track. Diane Coyle, along with Richard Baggaley, Sam Clark and Ellen White at London Publishing Partnership, provided invaluable editorial input.

Last but not least, our special thanks are due to Christoph Woermann and Clarissa Dann at Deutsche Bank. Without their inspiration the book would never have happened. They encouraged us to write this and, although the narrative and content are all ours, they convinced us that the weaponized trade message was important enough to reinforce in a second book.

Endnotes

1. R. Harding and J. Harding. 2017. *The Weaponization of Trade: The Great Unbalancing of Politics and Economics*. London: London Publishing Partnership.

2. *Economist*. 2019. America is deploying a new economic arsenal to assert its power, that is counterproductive and dangerous. 6 June (https://econ.st/2JYZqCh).

3. E. Schmidt and J. Cohen. 2014. *The New Digital Age: Reshaping the Future of People, Nations and Business*. London: John Murray Publishers.

4. World Trade Organization. 2018. *World Trade Statistical Review 2018* (https://bit.ly/2BXcmnj).

5. See https://www.oecd.org/trade/topics/digital-trade/.

6. N. Bose and A. Shalal. 2019. Trump says China is 'killing us with unfair trade deals'. Reuters, 7 August (https://reut.rs/2P22nVK).

7. C. Walker and J. Ludwig. 2017. The meaning of sharp power: how authoritarian states project influence. *Foreign Affairs*, 16 November (https://fam.ag/2z6AxPP).

8. Philip Hammond, in comments during a televised interview at an International Monetary Fund (IMF) meeting in Washington (https://bbc.in/2PjfiD9).

9. D. G. Brennan. 1971. Strategic alternatives: I. *The New York Times*. 24 May (page 31): https://nyti.ms/2P4d1LU.

10. L. Kudlow. 2019. Keynote address at US EXIM Bank's annual conference, Washington, DC, 28 March.

11. Speech to the Royal Institute of International Affairs, London. See https://bit.ly/2LqjTAC.

12. K. Davenport. June 2019. *Nuclear Weapons: Who Has What at a Glance*. Washington, DC: Arms Control Association (https://bit.ly/1P4O892).

13. Trump Twitter Archive (accessed 2 July 2019): https://bit.ly/33vWLWW.

14. G.W. Harrison and E.E. Rutström. 1991. Trade wars, trade negotiations and applied game theory. *The Economic Journal* 101(406): 420–435. Published by Wiley on behalf of the Royal Economic Society.

15. T.C. Schelling. 1960. *The Strategy of Conflict*. Cambridge, MA: Harvard University Press. Schelling argues that conflict, where it is pathological rather than inevitable, is rare but leads to a winner takes all approach to negotiations.

16. Schelling (1960): page 4.

17. See https://twitter.com/realDonaldTrump/status/969525362580484098.

18. See https://bloom.bg/2K7WS3T.

19. See https://bit.ly/30Jp2I6.

20. See Rebecca Harding's *GTR+ MENA* and *GTR+ Africa* reports (2019): https://bit.ly/3014YAi.

21. G. Rachman. 2019. Donald Trump is making America scary again. *Financial Times*, 10 June (https://on.ft.com/2WtqQ4Y).

22. H. Farrell and A. Newman. 2019. *Weaponized Interdependence*. Draft (https://bit.ly/2ZNwq4j).

23. J.A. Schumpeter. 2003. *Capitalism, Socialism and Democracy*. Taylor and Francis Online.

24. C. Perez. 2010. Technological revolutions and techno-economic paradigms. *Cambridge Journal of Economics* 34(1): 185–202.

25. C. Freeman and F. Luoçã. 2001. *As Time Goes By: From the Industrial Revolution to the Information Revolution*. Oxford: Oxford University Press.

26. Schmidt and Cohen (2014): page 3.

27. M. Smith. 2019. Most Conservative members would see party destroyed to achieve Brexit. *YouGov*, June 18 (https://bit.ly/2KYZu4G).

28. Schelling (1960).

29. See https://bit.ly/2N0ZtxO.

30. Farrell and Newman (2019).

31. See T.L. Friedman. 2007. *The World is Flat – The Globalized World in the 21st Century*. London: Penguin. See also D. Coyle. 1998. *The Weightless World: Strategies for Managing the Digital Economy*. Cambridge, MA and London: MIT Press.

32. SWIFT stands for the Society for Worldwide Interbank Financial Telecommunication. It was founded in 1973 to provide a standardized mechanism for interbank financial transfers.

33. C. Bildt and M. Leonard. 2019. From plaything to player: how Europe can stand up for itself in the next five years. Policy Brief, 17 July, European Council on Foreign Relations (https://bit.ly/2Y618Zb).

34. T.J. Wright. 2017. *All Measures Short of War: The Contest for the 21st Century and the Future of American Power*. New Haven, CT and London: Yale University Press.

35. R. Baldwin. 2019. *The Globotics Upheaval: Globalization, Robotics and the Future of Work*. London: Weidenfeld and Nicholson.

36. Wright (2017): page xi.

37. Baldwin (2019): page 5.

38. See F. Fukuyama. 1992. *The End of History and the Last Man*. London: Penguin. See also K. Ohmae. 1996. *The End of the Nation State: The Rise of the Regional Economies*. London: Harper Collins. See also S.P. Huntington. 1996. *The Clash of Civilizations and the Remaking of World Order*. London: Simon & Schuster.

39. J. Stiglitz. 2003. Globalization and the economic role of the state in the new millennium. *Industrial and Corporate Change* 12(1): 3–26 (https://doi.org/10.1093/icc/12.1.3).

40. J. Stiglitz. 2017. The overselling of globalization. *Business Economics* 52(3): 129–137 (https://bit.ly/2Z3rB62).

41. Freeman and Luoçã (2001): page 366.

42. T. Marshall. 2015. *Prisoners of Geography: Ten Maps that Tell You Everything You Need to Know about Global Politics*. London: Elliot and Thompson.

43. S. Paterson. 2018. *China, Trade and Power: Why the West's Economic Engagement Has Failed*. London: London Publishing Partnership.

44. See https://cnn.it/2IhqOBL.

45. See https://bit.ly/2COUvwk.

46. See *Strong and Secure: A Strategy for Australia's National Security*: https://bit.ly/301qhls.

47. Kudlow (2019).

48. See https://bit.ly/2MguZs6.

49. See https://bit.ly/2QXt8GA.

50. See https://bit.ly/2D6oIcx.

51. See https://bit.ly/2iVrkSQ.

52. See https://bit.ly/30Jp2I6.

53. See https://bit.ly/2CzLLd7.

54. See https://bit.ly/2CzLLd7.

55. B. Dudley. 2019. Why the US deficit keeps growing. *Bloomberg Opinion*, 15 March (https://bloom.bg/2YO3ZTe).

56. See https://bit.ly/2bTLIVC.

57. D. Simon. 2012. But did you see the gorilla? The problem with inattentional blindness. *Smithsonian.com*, September (https://bit.ly/2TDnVXH).

58. C.S. Gray. 2010. *The Strategy Bridge: Theory for Practice.* Oxford: Oxford University Press.

59. C. von Clausewitz. 1832 (1976). *On War.* Princeton, NJ: Princeton University Press, page 86.

60. See D. Bromwich. 1992. *Politics By Other Means: Higher Education and Group Thinking.* London: Yale University Press. See also B. Parks, S.W. Pharr and B.D. Lockeman. 1994. A marketer's guide to Clausewitz: lessons for winning market share. *Business Horizons* 37(4): 68–73 (accessed 24 June 2019).

61. R.M. Martin. 1847. *China: Political, Commercial, and Social; In an Official Report to Her Majesty's Government*, Volume 2. London: James Madden, pages 80–82.

62. A. Hirschman. 1945. *National Power and the Structure of Foreign Trade.* Oakland, CA: University of California Press, page 13.

63. Clausewitz (1832/1976): I: 1,24.

64. See https://bit.ly/2H14BhB.

65. See J. von Neumann. 1928. Zur Theorie der Gesellschaftsspiele. *Mathematische Annalen* 100(1): 295–320 (page 303). See also W. Poundstone. 1992. *Prisoner's Dilemma: John von Neumann, Game Theory, and the Puzzle of the Bomb.* New York, NY: Anchor Books, page 53.

66. C.S. Gray. 2016. *Strategy and Politics.* Oxford: Routledge, page 16.

67. B. de Jomini (trans. Captain G.H. Mendell and Lieutenant W.P. Craighill). 1862. *The Art of War.* Philadelphia, PA: J.B. Lippincott & Co, page 18.

68. B.L. Hart. 1967. *Strategy: The Indirect Approach.* London: Faber & Faber, page 17.

69. Wright (2017): page xi.

70. H. Kahn. 1962 (1984). *Thinking about the Unthinkable*. New York, NY: Simon & Schuster, page 21.

71. See J. Brander and B. Spencer. 1985. Export subsidies and international market share rivalry. *Journal of International Economics* 18: 83–100. See also B. Spencer and J. Brander. 1983. International R&D rivalry and industrial strategy. *Review of Economic Studies* 50: 707–722.

72. P. Krugman. 1986. Pricing to market when the exchange rate changes. Working Paper No. 1926, National Bureau of Economic Research.

73. Harding and Harding (2017): pages 5–7.

74. M. Handel. 1996. *Masters of War: Classical Strategic Thought*, 2nd edn. London: Frank Cass, page 36.

75. See https://bit.ly/2KHqzHL.

76. A. Moody. 2017. President Xi Jinping's global vision for China. *The Telegraph*, 9 November (https://bit.ly/2OUUGkb).

77. J.S. Nye, Jr. 2005. The rise of China's soft power. *Wall Street Journal Asia*, 29 December.

78. Pew Research Center. 14 July 2014. Chapter 2: China's image. In *Global Opposition to US Surveillance and Drones, but Limited Harm to America's Image* (https://pewrsr.ch/31Hap8d).

79. H. Gardner (ed. G. Lasconjarias and J.A. Larsen). 2015. *NATO's Response to Hybrid Threats*. Rome: NATO Defense College, page 169.

80. D. Blumenthal. 2018. Economic coercion as a tool in China's grand strategy. Statement, 24 July, American Enterprise Institute (https://bit.ly/2YFFOdU).

81. Coriolis Technologies, multilateral data.

82. S. Coll. 2004. *Ghost Wars: The Secret History of the CIA, Afghanistan and Bin Laden, from the Soviet Invasion to September 10, 2001*. London: Penguin, page 11.

83. R.O. Keohane and J.S. Nye, Jr. (ed. R.L. Betts). 2017. *Power and Interdependence* in *Conflict after the Cold War: Arguments on Causes of War and Peace*, 5th edn. New York, NY: Taylor & Francis, page 169.

84. Office of the White House. December 2017. *National Security Strategy of the United States of America*, page 4 (https://bit.ly/2CzLLd7).

85. Moody (2017).

86. Russian Federation President. December 2015. *Russian National Security Strategy*, chapter III, paragraph 30 (https://bit.ly/1SfWS0T).

87. B. Brodie. 1973. *War and Politics*. New York, NY: Macmillan, pages 452f.

88. Clausewitz (1832/1976): pages 13–15.

89. See S. Masayoshi. 2005. *A Journey in Search of the Origins of Go*. Santa Monica, CA: Yutopian Enterprises, pages 23–24. See also E. Lasker. 1934 (1960). *Go and Go-Moku*. Mineola, NY: Dover Publications.

90. P. Sabin. 2012. *Simulating War: Studying Conflict through Simulation Games*. London: Bloomsbury Publishing, page xv.

91. B. von Reisswitz. 1824 (1983). *Kriegsspiel: Instructions for the Representation of Military Manoeuvres with the Kriegsspiel Apparatus*. Hemel Hempstead: Bill Leeson.

92. M. van Creveld. 2013. *Wargames: From Gladiators to Gigabytes*. Cambridge: Cambridge University Press.

93. Clausewitz was also keen to highlight the futility of such academic exercises, as – faced with the reality of war – 'the light of reason is refracted in a manner quite different from that which is normal in academic speculation'. See Clausewitz (1832/1976): page 62.

94. P.P. Perla. 1990. *The Art of Wargaming: A Guide for Professionals and Hobbyists*. Annapolis, MD: Naval Institute Press, page 26.

95. Poundstone (1992): page 38.

96. Ibid.

97. J. von Neumann and O. Morgenstern. 1944. *Theory of Games and Economic Behaviour*. Princeton, NJ: Princeton University Press, page 31.

98. Neumann and Morgenstern (1944): page 30.

99. Neumann (1928): page 303.

100. See the definition of the 'Prisoner's Dilemma' on the *Stanford Encyclopedia of Philosophy* website: https://stanford.io/2gWRNZT.

101. Schelling (1960): pages 83–84.

102. T.C. Schelling. 2010. Game theory: a practitioner's approach. *Economics and Philosophy* 26(1): 27–46.

103. T.C. Schelling. 16 April 1958 (rev. 28 May 1958). *The Reciprocal Fear of Surprise Attack*. Santa Monica, CA: The RAND Corporation, page 1.

104. Sabin (2012): page 11.

105. Neumann and Morgenstern (1944): pages 15–31.

106. A. Rapoport. 1974. *Conflict in Man-Made Environment*. Baltimore, MD: Penguin.

107. J. Snyder. 1977. *The Soviet Strategic Culture: Implications for Limited Nuclear Operations*. Report, RAND Corporation, page 8.

108. Ibid.

109. A phrase coined by Alastair Iain Johnson in his essay: A.I. Johnson. 1995. Thinking about strategic culture. *International Security* 19(4): 32–64.

110. C.S. Gray. 1999. Strategic culture as context: the first generation of theory strikes back. *Review of International Studies* 25(1): 49–69 (page 50).

111. C.S. Gray. 1981. National styles in strategy: the American example. *International Security* 6(2): 21–47 (page 22).

112. C. Lord. 1985. American strategic culture. *Comparative Strategy* 5(3): 269–293 (page 272).

113. Gray (1999): page 50.

114. Ibid., page 52.

115. S. Poore. 2003. What is the context? A reply to the Gray–Johnston debate on strategic culture. *Review of International Studies* 29(2): 279–284 (page 281).

116. S. Lantis. 2009. Strategic culture and tailored deterrence: bridging the gap between theory and practice. *Contemporary Security Policy* 30(3): 467–485.

117. B. Heuser. 1998. *Nuclear Mentalities? Strategies and Beliefs in Britain, France and the FRG*. Basingstoke: Macmillan Press Limited, page 1.

118. Clausewitz (1832/1976): page 141.

119. P. Navarro. 2019. Keynote speech at US EXIM Bank's annual conference, Washington, DC, 28 March (https://bit.ly/2ZZzWJf).

120. Colonel William Braun, cited in: D. Vergun. 2016. Ancient game used to understand US–China strategy. *US Army News*, 24 May (https://bit.ly/2KWEycX).

121. From the *Washington Post* article 'A tie is like kissing your sister', published 9 November 1953 (page 12): https://bit.ly/1HOGeKs.

122. *National Security Strategy of the United States of America* (December 2017): pages 28–29.

123. N. Akpan. 2016. Google artificial intelligence beats champion at world's most complicated board game. *PBS News Hour*, 27 January (https://to.pbs.org/300lWyH).

124. The full text of Sun Tzu's *The Art of War* can be found at https://bit.ly/2OUUn9b.

125. H. Kissinger. 2011. *On China*. London: Penguin, page 29.

126. D. Hofstadter. May 1983. The Prisoner's Dilemma: computer tournaments and the evolution of cooperation. In *Metamagical Themas*. New York, NY: Basic Books, pages 715–734 (page 721): https://bit.ly/33vxZGp.

127. E. Simpson. 2016. The contributions of Anatol Rapoport to game theory. Working Paper 135, Political Science Publications, pages 16–18 (https://bit.ly/2YWXq0g).

128. G. Rachman. 2019. Brexit is an idea for a bygone era. *Financial Times*, 24 June (https://on.ft.com/2KIh0bB).

129. EXIM. 2018. *Report to the US Congress on Global Export Credit Competition* (https://bit.ly/2TsxVmo).

130. See https://time.com/5444680/jack-ma-trade-war/.

131. Wright (2017): page 5.

132. Ibid., page 16.

133. R. Baldwin. 2016. *The Great Convergence: Information Technology and the New Globalization*. Cambridge, MA: Harvard University Press.

134. Wright (2017): pages 17–18.

135. G. Magnus. 2018. *Red Flags: Why Xi's China is in Jeopardy*. New Haven, CT and London: Yale University Press.

136. R. Brooks. 2016. *How Everything Became War and the Military Became Everything: Tales from the Pentagon*. New York, NY: Simon & Schuster.

137. *National Security Strategy of the United States of America* (December 2017): page 2.

138. *National Security Strategy of the United States of America* (December 2017).

139. Navarro (2019).

140. Ibid.

141. See https://bloom.bg/2ZZFWBL.

142. P.D. Gewirtz. 2019. Can the US–China crisis be stabilized? As US–China relations reach a crisis point, strategic thinking is dangerously absent. *Brookings Institute*, 26 June (https://brook.gs/2KA5Dnj).

143. Navarro (2019).

144. See https://bit.ly/2BGsNm9, https://bit.ly/2QG7N4s, https://bit.ly/2T6pD6N and https://bit.ly/2u2bQhD.

145. Harding and Harding (2017): page 94.

146. See https://bit.ly/2Y5BJyl.

147. See https://bit.ly/2Nk2PZk.

148. See https://reut.rs/2F12Q2Z.

149. Magnus (2018).

150. Ibid.

151. J. McBride and A. Chatzky. 2019. Is 'Made in China 2025' a threat to global trade? Council on Foreign Relations, 13 May (https://on.cfr.org/2M4nFQ9).

152. A. Trevidi. 2018. China's Made in 2025 plan is a paper tiger. *Bloomberg Opinion*, 16 December (https://bloom.bg/2MdrqTy).

153. E. Blaauw. 2013. The driving forces behind China's foreign policy: has China become more assertive? Economics Discussion Paper, 23 October, Rabobank (https://bit.ly/31Fi06T).

154. The full speech can be found at https://bit.ly/2Kt01Jt.

155. Coface Country Risk Conference, June 2019.

156. Harding and Harding (2017).

157. G.F. Kennan. 1960. Peaceful coexistence: a Western view. Foreign Relations, January (https://fam.ag/2KMsOJB).

158. See https://bit.ly/2qTxfsF.

159. Magnus (2018).

160. See https://bit.ly/2TvbMlR.

161. See https://mck.co/2aeQW8L.

162. See https://bit.ly/2qeTtq3.

163. See https://bit.ly/31CbNZt.

164. See https://bit.ly/2Am42y2.

165. T. Rühling. 2019. A 'new' Chinese foreign policy under Xi Jinping? Focus Asia Report, Institute for Security and Development Policy (https://bit.ly/2Z0ET7q).

166. See https://bit.ly/2vZbCut.

167. Ibid.

168. D.R. Palmer. 2015. Back to the future? Russia's hybrid warfare, revolutions in military affairs, and Cold War comparisons. Research Paper 120, October, NATO Defense College, Rome, page 2.

169. P. Tsygankov. 2015. Gibridnyye Voyny: ponyatiya, interpretatsii i real'nost' [Hybrid wars: definitions, interpretations and reality]. In P. Tsygankov (ed.) *Gibridnyye Voyny' v khaotiziruyushchemsya mire XXI veka* [Hybrid Wars in the Chaotic World of the 21st Century]. Moscow, Moscow University Press, page 21.

170. European Council. 2019. *Association Agreement between the European Union and its Member States, of the one part, and Ukraine, of the other part.* Available at https://bit.ly/2VGhAuR (accessed 22 October 2018; it has since been updated).

171. V. Shevchenko. 2014. 'Little Green Men' or 'Russian Invaders'? *BBC*, 11 March (https://bbc.in/31JLdh2).

172. V. Gerasimov. 2013. The value of science in foresight: new challenges require re-thinking the forms and methods of warfare. *VPK News*, 26 February (https://vpk-news.ru/articles/14632): accessed 5 November 2018.

173. C.K. Bartles. 2016. Getting Gerasimov right. *Military Review* January/ February: 30–38 (page 34).

174. Alexei Alexeyevich Venediktov interview by vDud (вДудь), 13 March 2018 (https://bit.ly/2Dp90q6): accessed 5 November 2018. Venediktov is a journalist and moderate opposition voice to Russia's regime. He gave his opinion on Putin's strategic objectives in an interview in Spring 2018, where he spoke of the emergence of a new Putin since the latter's Munich speech in 2007, in which he railed against US hegemony and the unipolar world order. Venediktov claims that to view Putin as a 'reactionary restorer': someone who believes what was done for 20 years before he became president was the wrong way, while the 'right way is what happened long before the beginning of "perestroika", long before the start of transformation, even before the Soviet Union'. Putin's goal, according to Venediktov, is to restore an empire in order to challenge US hegemony, an outcome that is 'better for everyone and better for the world, because when two empires, the United States and ... Russia, stand on two legs, the world is more stable'.

175. Ibid.

176. Gerasimov (2013): accessed 5 November 2018.

177. Ibid.

178. See https://bit.ly/1Zu580D (accessed 4 November 2018).

179. Gerasimov (2013): accessed 5 November 2018.

180. J. Yazigi. 2014. Syria's war economy. Policy Brief, European Council on Foreign Relations (https://bit.ly/2N3piO6).

181. See pages 2–3 of the article 'Game changer: Russian sub-launched cruise missiles bring strategic effect', available at https://bit.ly/2KyBEvZ.

182. T. Nilsen. 2019. Russian sub launched cruise missile without leaving port. *The Barents Observer*, April 3.

183. A. Stent. 2014. Putin's Ukrainian endgame and why the West may have a hard time stopping him. *CNN*, March 4 (https://cnn.it/2Mh6F9A): accessed 6 November 2018.

184. O. Shchedrov and C. Lowe. 2008. Russia army vows steps if Georgia and Ukraine join NATO. *Reuters*, April 11 (https://reut.rs/2Z0XbRH): accessed 6 November 2018.

185. Source: Coriolis Technologies.

186. See the 2013 article 'Putin says Ukraine–EU deal a threat to Russia', *Al Jazeera*, 27 November (https://bit.ly/2Z1thAP): accessed 22 October 2018.

187. OHCHR. 13 June 2019. *Report on the Human Rights Situation in Ukraine 16 February to 15 May 2019*. UN Office of the High Commissioner for Human Rights (https://bit.ly/2MXNQbb).

188. Bold in original. See https://bit.ly/1uf9LFM.

189. J. Bender. 2014. Here are all the Russian weapons separatists are using in Ukraine. *Business Insider*, 21 November (https://bit.ly/2NcwOGv).

190. See AK74, 18 August 2018. https://alchetron.com/AK-74.

191. See https://bit.ly/2MeMY28.

192. C.J. Chivers. 2014. In Ukraine, spent cartridges offer clues to violence fueled by Soviet surplus. *The New York Times*, 24 July (https://nyti.ms/2H6NISM): accessed 19 December 2018.

193. See Resolution 2231 (2015) of the United Nations Security Council, adopted at its 7488th meeting on 20 July 2015: S/RES/2231 (2015), page 1.

194. B.B. Taleblu. 2018. Iranian ballistic missile tests since the nuclear deal – 2.0. Report, January 25, Foundation for Defense of Democracies, page 11: https://bit.ly/2Kyc3mN.

195. M. Elleman and M. Fitzpatrick. 2018. Assessing whether Iran's ballistic missiles are designed to be nuclear-capable. *International Institute for Strategic Studies*, 28 February: pages 4 and 23.

196. *Russian National Security Strategy*, article 17.

197. Elleman and Fitzpatrick (2018): page 22.

198. The full transcript of Trump's speech on the Iran nuclear deal can be found at https://nyti.ms/2KK1qeN.

199. A. Ward. 2019. Rouhani: Iran to stay in Iran nuclear deal – for now. *Vox*, 8 May (https://bit.ly/33xRqyr).

200. Editorial. 2019. US sends aircraft carrier and bomber task force to 'warn Iran'. *BBC*, 6 May (https://bbc.in/2H5oDru).

201. S. Holland and P. Hafezi. 2019. Trump threatens 'obliteration', Iran calls White House 'mentally retarded'. *Reuters*, 25 June (https://reut.rs/2X9dD6g).

202. A. Smith and S. Kim. 2019. Trump's Iran policy is deepening mistrust in North Korea, experts say. *NBC News*, 29 June (https://nbcnews.to/2Jg71cx).

203. V. Pop. 2019. Europe plans no immediate sanctions if Iran breaches nuclear deal. *The Wall Street Journal*, 29 June (https://on.wsj.com/2YmfxgC).

204. L. Morris. 2019. US tells Europe: choose between us and Iran, as new trading system launches. *Washington Post*, 28 June (https://wapo.st/2yW0PBJ).

205. Soviet general Georgy Zhukov quoted in: D.D. Eisenhower. 1963. *Mandate for Change, 1953–1956: The White House Years*. New York, NY: Doubleday, page 518.

206. For the Treaty of Rome, see https://bit.ly/2xPs8Of.

207. For the Single European Act, see https://bit.ly/2MhkJ36.

208. Comments made during an internal session held for the European export credit agencies, London, 29 May 2019.

209. Industrie 4.0 was a German national strategy to enhance the country's digital competitiveness; it suggests there were tensions between national and Europe-wide digital interests as early as 2017: see https://bit.ly/2Gou9Tf.

210. The *National Security Strategy of the United States of America* (December 2017) refers to 'mercantilist trading blocs' generically to mean the North America Free Trade Area (NAFTA) and the European Union (EU) in particular.

211. See https://bit.ly/2ziGwgj.

212. See https://bit.ly/2KSrOX5.

213. The full text of the Minsk agreement can be found, translated, at https://on.ft.com/2puVeMg.

214. See https://bit.ly/2KyFy7X.

215. See https://bit.ly/2DWRY7G.

216. https://bit.ly/31OE1An.

217. See https://bit.ly/2Z3olHA.

218. See https://bit.ly/2hCt4jX.

219. See https://politi.co/2McJSvD.

220. L. Beraud-Sudreau. 2019. On the up: Western defence spending in 2018. *Institute for International Strategic Studies*, 15 February (https://bit.ly/33yP6ak).

221. See https://bit.ly/2Z1CQfk.

222. European Political Strategy Centre. 2019. EU industrial policy after Siemens–Alstrom. Report, European Commission (https://bit.ly/2KSrOX5).

223. See https://cnb.cx/2YM8xhr.

224. See https://on.ft.com/2LomM4I.

225. See https://bit.ly/2KvglLr.

226. C. Walker. 2018. What is sharp power? *Journal of Democracy* 29(3): 9–23 (https://bit.ly/2Kwm6oV).

227. W. Brandt. 1961. The means short of war. *Foreign Relations*, January (https://fam.ag/2N47ylt). Kissinger's analysis of the post-World War II period into the Cold War suggests that he saw the nuclear deterrent as a mechanism for creating a power struggle that, ultimately, would not involve direct war. His sentiments are articulated in this interview: https://on.cfr.org/33xnbYo. The title of Thomas J. Wright's 2017 book *All Means Short of War* (op cit.) reinforces the view that it has not been and shall not be the intention to go to war in the military sense of the word, but conflict remains inevitable and miscalculation likely.

228. Wright (2017): page xii.

229. See, for example, Wright (2017); A.-M. Slaughter. 2016. *The Chessboard and the Web: Strategies of Connection in a Networked World*. New Haven, CT: Yale University Press; and Brooks (2016).

230. P. Seabright. 2010. *The Company of Strangers: A Natural History of Economic Life*. Princeton, NJ: Princeton University Press.

231. See https://bit.ly/2daz7Yr.

232. M. Wolf. 2018. Facebook enters dangerous waters with Libra. *Financial Times*, 25 June (https://on.ft.com/31X7kBO).

233. International Chamber of Commerce. 2018. *Global Trade: Securing Future Growth* (https://bit.ly/2yXpjul).

234. N. McCarthy. 2018. 1.7 billion people in the world do not have access to a bank account. *Forbes*, 8 June (https://bit.ly/2OV7bw9).

235. W. Münchau. 2019. America's exorbitant privilege is Europe's sin of omission. *Financial Times*, 26 May (https://on.ft.com/2YYoiwZ).

236. See https://bit.ly/2x8VlFZ.

237. See https://bit.ly/2tytqut.

238. E. Wragg. 2019. Roundtable: driving consensus in sustainable trade finance. *Global Trade Review*, 23 April (https://bit.ly/2Tu8Vv9).